Catherine Gladstone

CATHERINE GLADSTONE

From Messrs. Nisbet's List

SOME HAWARDEN LETTERS
15/- net

Edited by LISLE MARCH PHILLIPPS and BERTRAM CHRISTIAN

A FORTY YEARS' FRIENDSHIP
10/6 net

Letters from Canon H. Scott Holland to Mrs. Drew. Edited by Canon OLLARD

W. G. C. GLADSTONE: A Memoir
5/- net

By VISCOUNT GLADSTONE

UNIV. OF
CALIFORNI

Mrs GLADSTONE

CATHERINE GLADSTONE

BY HER DAUGHTER
MARY DREW

London
NISBET & CO. LTD.
22 BERNERS STREET, W.1

CATHERINE GLADSTONE

BY HER DAUGHTER
MARY DREW

London
NISBET & CO. LTD.
22 BERNERS STREET, W.1

First Published in 1919

TO

THE DEAR AND HONOURED MEMORY

OF

MY MOTHER AND FATHER

AND TO

MY BROTHERS AND SISTERS

IN LOVE AND GRATITUDE

Prevent us, O Lord, in all our doings, with Thy most gracious favour; that in all our works begun, continued, and ended in Thee, we may glorify Thy holy Name; through Jesus Christ our Lord

INTRODUCTION

HAVING, a few years ago, written a sketch of my Mother for private circulation, by the wish of my brothers and sisters it was printed in 1916 in the *Cornhill Magazine*. So deep and unusual an interest was aroused in her life and personality, that the desire for fuller treatment, for more light on the picture, was expressed by those who have the best right to ask it. But it remains a sketch, and I have felt that in some cases a sketch really reveals more than a finished picture. It leaves more to the imagination.

It is a selection, made almost at random, from some among the scenes and incidents, the experiences and emotions, of her long life as they have occurred to her daughter. The book can hardly be called a monograph, for it seemed necessary to recall the atmosphere, the surroundings in which she lived and moved and had her being. For this reason I have touched on other lives than hers. It cannot be necessary to apologise for the abiding sense of her husband's presence, ever permeating her own being. It will be recognised that, if these glimpses into her life and times are to give a truthful portrait of her, it was necessary to study his personality as well as hers —in fact they were inseparable. For this the home daughter had, through life, exceptional opportunities; for, owing to the marriage of one sister in 1873 and the Cambridge career (1878–96) of the other (though naturally they were both much at home), she had the privilege of living with her parents both before and after her own marriage (1886), practically from her birth to their deaths.

I should wish to thank Mr. A. T. Bassett and Miss M'Carthy for their excellent secretarial help in dealing with the papers.

To Lord Morley I owe a debt of gratitude that can never be paid for the inspiration of his Biography.

M. D.

September 1919.

CONTENTS

		PAGE
INTRODUCTION	. . . .	vii

CHAP.		
I. CHILDHOOD AND YOUTH	. . .	1
II. GIRLHOOD AND MARRIAGE	. . .	24
III. EARLY DIARIES AND MARRIED LIFE	.	40
IV. LETTERS FROM HER	. . . .	75
V. LETTERS TO HER	. . . .	120
VI. CHARACTERISTICS	. . . .	202
VII. GOOD WORKS	. . . .	220
VIII. REMINISCENCES	. . . .	254
IX. "VIA CRUCIS—VIA LUCIS"	. .	282
GENEALOGICAL TABLE	. . .	293
INDEX	. . . . .	295

LIST OF ILLUSTRATIONS

Mrs. Gladstone	*Frontispiece*
	FACING PAGE
Venetia Stanley (Lady Digby)	4
Catherine, Mary, Stephen, and Henry Glynne at Audley End	8
Catherine and Mary Glynne	10
Sir Stephen Glynne	17
Hawarden Castle	28
Fasque	35
Mrs. Gladstone and her Sister, Lady Lyttelton, on the Lawn at Hawarden	42
Hagley Hall	68
Catherine Gladstone	87
Mary, Lady Lyttelton	89
Mrs. Gladstone and Herbert	102
Lady Braybrooke and Lady Fortescue	128
The Rt. Hon. W. E. Gladstone	148

LIST OF ILLUSTRATIONS

	FACING PAGE
A Family Group at Hawarden	186
Mrs. Gladstone at Hawarden	228
Billingbear	244
Mrs. Gladstone at Dollis Hill, with her Granddaughter, Dorothy Drew	260
Mr. and Mrs. Gladstone at Cannes	278
Hawarden Castle by Night	286

CATHERINE GLADSTONE

CHAPTER I

CHILDHOOD AND YOUTH

"WHO is that lady, and what is she doing?" The lady in question was Mrs. Gladstone; she was carrying babies rolled up in blankets from the London Hospital, at the time of the virulent outbreak of cholera in 1866.

Catherine Glynne was born at Hawarden Castle on January 6, 1812. Both her parents were descended from Crusaders. Her father, Sir Stephen Glynne, representative of the Percy Barony, was twenty-fourth in descent from William de Percy, a Norman chieftain who came over to England in 1066 with William the Conqueror. He accompanied Duke Robert to the Holy Land in the First Crusade, and died near Jerusalem in 1096.

Her mother, Mary Neville, daughter of Lord Braybrooke and Catherine Grenville, was eighteenth in descent from Richard de Grenville and Lady Isabelle, daughter of

Lord Buckingham. Richard de Grenville, a Crusader, died in the Holy Land in 1147. Mary Neville was related to five Prime Ministers—the two Grenvilles (one of whom was her grandfather), Lord Chatham, Mr. Pitt, and Mr. Gladstone, her son-in-law.

Mr. Gladstone compiled for the use of his children the list of the statesmen related to their grandmother, Lady Glynne:

Right Hon. George Grenville	Grandfather.
Sir William Wyndham	Great-Grandfather.
Lord Chatham	Great-Uncle.
Mr. Pitt	First Cousin.
Lord Grenville	Great-Uncle.
Lord Buckingham	Great-Uncle.

Proud she might have been of the great historic names among her ancestors. Mr. Gladstone, if the idea had appealed to her, would have liked the Percy title to have been re-created on her behalf, she being one of the representatives of the Percy Barony. But she never would have borne to take a name different from that of her husband. Through Agnes de Percy and Jocelyn de Louvaine, she was directly descended from Charlemagne. Both her parents were on the Plantagenet Roll. To select a few of the most famous names in the history of England—Egbert, William the Conqueror, Harry Hotspur, and Edward I. were among her ancestors. Sir Richard Grenville of glorious memory, the hero of Tennyson's "Revenge," was a member of her family.[1]

Sir John Glyn, Lord Chief Justice of England, second son of Sir William Glyn of Glynlifon, Carnarvonshire, was the founder of the Hawarden branch of the family. Being a younger son, he could not inherit the beautiful home of his Glyn ancestors. He went out into the world to seek his fortunes. He was twenty-first in descent from Cil Maen Troed Dhu, one of the seven Kings or Chieftains of Wales who flourished in 848.

This brilliant young barrister won his spurs during the indictment of Lord Strafford. His speech on that occasion changed the fortunes of the day, and resulted in the condemnation and death of Strafford. Sir John was buried beneath the Altar in St. Margaret's Church, Westminster. There was a decided fitness in the Glynnes following the Stanleys as owners of Hawarden,[2] Sir Stephen Glynne, father of Mrs. Gladstone, being fourth in descent from Venetia Stanley,[3] "the renowned beauty," granddaughter of Lord Derby; and

---

[1] Many families, of course, could claim the same historic descent, or others as notable. But there is a limit to those who, without personal research, can find it notified in standard works of genealogy.

[2] Glynlifon was acquired by the Wynns through marriage with the Glyn heiress.

[3] Venetia married Sir Kenelm Digby, whose fine portrait by Vandyck hangs over the chimney-piece in the Library at Hawarden Castle.

the Stanleys had intermarried with Catherine Glynne's ancestors.

Her father and mother were distinguished by remarkable beauty of face and form—beauty inherited by both their daughters. Their marriage was tragically cut short, after a few happy years, by Sir Stephen's death at the early age of thirty. They had posted to the Riviera as a last hope of benefiting his lungs. It is curious to read in Lady Glynne's journal that, there being then no professional nurses, any stray friend of hers staying at Nice—Lady Bradford and others—took it in turns to look after the patient. They had taken with them their carriages and riding horses, a whole retinue of servants, and the little eldest boy aged six.

Napoleon was then safe in captivity at Elba. They bought, probably for the use of the invalid, one of his famous white chargers,[1] the same horse which had carried him at the terrible battle of Borodino and in the succeeding stages of his retreat from Russia.

It was in the year of the battle of Waterloo that Sir Stephen's death took place. Lady Glynne was caught in the great Hundred Days. Napoleon had made his escape from Elba and was at large. Lord Braybrooke set

---

[1] This horse went with them to England, after the death of Sir Stephen, and eventually died and was buried at Hawarden.

VENETIA STANLEY (LADY DIGBY)
GREAT-GREAT-GREAT-GRANDMOTHER OF MRS. GLADSTONE
From Vandyck's portrait at Windsor

CALIFORNIA

off from England to escort his daughter home, but his coach was stopped and his horses commandeered.

Meanwhile Lady Glynne was advised not to travel by sea for fear of the ship being seized and interned. They contrived to reach Genoa safely, and thence, with many complications, they posted across Lombardy, Switzerland, and Flanders on their way to England.

With her four children, all under six, this beautiful young widow returned to the home of her girlhood, and lived with her father in London, at Audley End, and at Billingbear. For three months of each year she resided at Hawarden. There is a diary in existence containing notes on her children between 1815 and 1822. Catherine, at the age of three, is mentioned as a magnificent specimen with curly golden hair, abounding in animal spirits, a coaxing, passionate little Pussy. She sometimes " pretends to be feminine—' Pussy so fightened,' she says, when having no notion of fear." At four she says, " Nothin's too dood for Mammy." She had a passion for her aunt, Lady Chatham: laid hold of her and held her tight on her departure from Audley End—" Don't go, dear Chat "—and was unwilling to let her get into the carriage.

At five, she reads nicely and begins to write, knows a little French and geography, showed great pluck over the extraction of a double tooth, minding far more when her brother Henry's was drawn. " Blooming and healthy as it is possible for a child to be, devoted to her sister and brothers, much attracted by dress and finery, a beautiful child, but Mary may still grow up to be the prettiest."

January 1818.—" Catherine, just six, reads and writes nicely. Learns a page of Bible History by heart. She has been in several passions lately. The great punishment—dining by herself on Christmas Day, when I dined with the other children and George[1] and Charlotte—will, I trust, prevent their so frequent recurrence; for she is really good and docile in general, picks up quickly."

The accounts of her elder brother Stephen are more detailed, so interesting and unique was his character. The French governess who arrived in April 1818 brings improvement to Catherine's manners. She has music lessons at six and a half, and would sit for hours listening to music—" fewer passions, and in general good and affectionate. A nice little voice and a true ear. She is a very good horsewoman." There are many health details

[1] The Rev. and Hon. George Neville Grenville, Rector of Hawarden. His wife was Lady Charlotte Legge.

and much about physic, emetics being the order of the day. Mary at seven is described as witty and extremely entertaining, rattles away in French. Catherine loves reading, and the list of histories they read in French would frighten parents of the present day. The diary ends abruptly, September 1822.

Their education was probably rather unusual, but must have been wisely conducted. A series of long-suffering governesses were possibly not of much good, but Lady Glynne was a remarkably clever, cultivated woman, as is shown by her letters. Catherine spoke Italian and French with ease and fluency, and the former with a beautiful accent. She had an extraordinary memory for poetry, and could easily, even in much later years, beat any of us in the game of " capping verses "— chiefly from the classics, Pope and Milton and Shakespeare. She surprised us all one evening late in life by repeating by heart Mazzini's great ode to Napoleon, the " Cinque Maggio." She had some knowledge of Latin, and could construe stray passages for us. Certainly she read little in later life—one was not accustomed to seeing a book or even a newspaper in her hand—but her books of extracts testify to very serious reading in her youth; the mere fact of her reading Mr. Gladstone's first book, *The Church in its Relations with the*

State, before he became her devout lover, testifies to her resolution. There are long extracts from Newman's *Sermons*, and later on we read a passage from St. Augustine in Mr. Gladstone's handwriting. She was in the habit of reading aloud to her children in later years: Scott's novels were read in that way.

The following little note written in retrospect by Catherine is interesting for its words on Bishop Heber, a great friend of Lady Glynne's:

"I could not have been more than eight when Bishop Heber first visited Hawarden Castle—1820, I believe—but words spoken of him by my mother have not faded. In 1815 she had become a widow. It was natural at this time of trial that intercourse such as was now offered should be of special value to her. For I recall the Bishop's singular gifts, his greatness, his charm, his persuasiveness. So it was through her conversation afterwards that I can recall how comforting and precious it was to her. Then I remember the deep interest on hearing that he was to be Bishop of Calcutta, and the awe and sadness with which we received the tidings of his death."

Long afterwards Mrs. Gladstone told her daughter she remembered how much startled

CATHERINE, MARY, STEPHEN, AND HENRY GLYNNE
AT AUDLEY END

From a coloured drawing by Eden U. Eddis

and grieved her mother (Lady Glynne) had been when she received an offer of marriage from one of her friends after she became a widow. In all her youth and beauty she had a sense of absolute consecration after the death of her husband. With so strong a feeling on her own part, she fully expected others to realise the same.

Catherine's aunt, Lady Wenlock, left it on record "that as a child it was difficult to teach her, and that she was recalcitrant in learning any kind of 'lessons'" [just what one would have guessed in after life from her impatience of routine]. "But nobody ever thought this implied any lack of intelligence. The fact was, she was immensely interested in life at first hand, and she refused to take her knowledge from other people's brains or books."

In 1828 when her daughters had reached the ages of fifteen and sixteen, Lady Glynne took them with their governess to Paris. This was with the object of education, and among their masters was the great Abbé Liszt, who taught them the pianoforte. Though still in the schoolroom, Lady Glynne was persuaded to take them to two or three special festivities. No sooner had they set foot in Paris than Lord Douglas (their brother Henry's greatest friend) arrived at their hotel to plead with

Lady Glynne to bring them to his mother's[1] dance. On hearing that the entertainment was partly for children, Lady Glynne, to the intense delight of the Pussies, consented to bring them. The hairdresser was sent for. "Just as mine was begun," wrote the elder Puss, " Stephen presented me with a bouquet in jewelry, the precious stones forming little flowers, the prettiest thing you ever saw; it is now fixed in my hair, and is facing Mama, who cannot take her eyes off it." All fright on the part of the girls was dispelled by the great kindness of the Duchess's welcome, and Lord Douglas opened the ball with Catherine.

But the Palais Royal was evidently considered too grown up, and Catherine describes in a letter to Henry how her mother, accompanied by her eldest son,[2] attended the ball given by the Duc d'Orléans. They were dazzled by the grandeur of the rooms and the brilliance of the company, though dismayed by the throng. The prettiest sight of all, writes Catherine, was when the door opened and the Duchesse de Berri attended by a bevy of damsels all came dancing into the room in fancy dress, " like opera dancers, sixteen in number, the prettiest thing Mama ever saw. They

---

[1] Eldest son of the Duke of Hamilton; one of the most romantic and fascinating figures of that day.
[2] Sir Stephen Glynne, then nineteen years of age.

CATHERINE AND MARY GLYNNE
AGED 17 AND 18
From a drawing by J. Slater at Hawarden

UNIV. OF
CALIFORNIA

formed into a quadrille. They had little black shoes with gold bows, and fancy dresses; the music was beautiful with Tyrolean tunes, and the *Gunters*[1] who handed the refreshments were all in dress coats with swords. Mama and Ste. were fortunate in escaping at twelve, by a little back door, and were amused at getting a peep of the cooks, who all appeared dog tired."

They were also allowed to attend Lady Stuart de Rothsay's ball at the British Embassy, and one or two more special dances; Mary, to her great delight, being taken to the Opera to hear Malibran, to make up for not always accompanying her sister. Lady Stuart's beautiful daughters, afterwards Lady Canning and Lady Waterford, became great friends with the Pussies. Stephen attended a Court and was presented to the King. "His coat was a pretty brown, with cut steel buttons and lace ruffles and frills, black satin shorts and white silk stockings. With Mama's sapphire and diamond brooch fastened in the lace, and his hair nicely dressed, he looked very well," writes Catherine to Henry. She mentions one of her partners, Lord Aboyne—the Lord Aboyne who had actually danced with Marie Antoinette—"he danced as if he were twenty instead of seventy. Brides

[1] The hired waiters.

dance as much as anyone, and age appears as no reason for not dancing."

Though still in the schoolroom, they had a gay time in Paris: they danced with the young bloods, both English and foreign, of the day, about whom they wrote, full of girlish rapture, to their brother Henry, preparing for Oxford at his tutor's house.

Lady Glynne, in her loneliness, leant much upon her uncle, Mr. Thomas Grenville, and still more upon her brother, George Neville Grenville, Rector of Hawarden. The latter came to Hawarden in 1813, shortly before the death of his brother-in-law, Sir Stephen Glynne. He was ordained Deacon and Priest on two succeeding days, and bad as was the old system of pitchforking any son or near kinsman of the house into the family living, irrespective of fitness, it was a good day for the huge parish of Hawarden when this very youthful Rector took charge. The parish of Hawarden was about the largest in the kingdom. It contained fifteen townships and now includes eight or nine churches. It was a Peculiar, *i.e.* not under the jurisdiction of a Bishop. If a Bishop's presence was required, as for Confirmation, he was invited as a guest, the Rector standing at the church door and welcoming him. But he was careful to define the business of the Bishop as confined to the performance of the one act—the laying on of hands. In great state, the Rector held a yearly Court in a chapel divided from the church. Here he proved wills, granted marriage licences, etc., and dealt with the conduct of his parishioners. He awarded punishment for lapses from orthodoxy and virtue—also for minor offences, such as sleeping or misbehaving in church or in its precincts. Public confession was the usual penalty. In 1850, sixteen years after Henry Glynne became Rector, these privileged Courts were abolished by Act of Parliament, but certain special powers still remain. Up to 1818 Hawarden had chiefly been notorious for its bad conduct. The first act of the new young Rector was to call his parishioners together: "I cannot change your hearts," he said to them, "that has to be done by yourselves with the help of God, but I can lessen your temptations." And accordingly he and Lady Glynne started in good earnest and did away with various public-houses on the estate, and established a rule which went far to anticipate the Sunday Closing Act. They were autocrats in those days. Two new churches were built in Hawarden parish during his rectorship; schools were established in Hawarden and its districts, which flourished chiefly through the bounty and energetic help and sympathy of Lady Glynne and later of her sons and daughters. Queen Victoria, who with her mother, the Duchess of Kent, visited Hawarden Castle so long ago as 1832, mentioned only a short time before she died, to a member of the family, how well she remembered the " beautiful Miss Glynnes." She first met them at Bishopthorpe. Many were the young men that frequented the parties at Hawarden, and on the Duke of Cambridge the impression left by his visit was more than ordinary; his friendship with Mrs. Gladstone only ended with his death.

The sisters were brought up with infinite and most loving care and discipline, duty being always placed before pleasure. Reticence and self-control, in those days, were considered indispensable to good manners and good breeding. Not so much the condescending life, as the sense of brotherhood, the lifting up of their friends, whether rich or poor, to their own level; thinking more of others than of themselves—this was the essence of the lady, the significance of *noblesse oblige*. And in their hearts was the love and fear of God— " the beginning of wisdom." In these days of personal service, when inspiring examples and writings have kindled the enthusiasm and self-sacrifice of so many, the character and aims of these sisters would not perhaps be as uncommon as in the earlier years of the nineteenth century.

Every year three or four families, specially intimate with one another, were accustomed, about Christmas time, to assemble by turns at each other's country homes—Hawarden Castle, Vale Royal, Acton Park, and Norton Priory. The lovely daughters of Sir Richard Brooke, famous for their beauty, were ever the dearest friends of the Glynnes. On these occasions they met for the acting of plays: their refreshments, on the evening of any special performance, consisted of cold custard and glasses of milk flavoured with nutmeg—rather a contrast to modern habits. In later days, at Hawarden and Hagley, there were yearly plays acted by the sons and daughters.

Both the sisters were excellent horsewomen and greatly skilled with the bow and arrow. Archery parties, or bow meetings, as they were called in Wales, were the craze of that day—a pretty and graceful pastime needing great skill. Great was the competition between the country houses in the neighbourhood of Hawarden. They visited their relations and friends, and many of the pleasantest country houses of England were open to the family through the ties of kinship—Audley End, Stowe, Vale Royal, Wynnstay, Powderham, Dropmore, Boconoc, Escrich, Billingbear, etc.

But the first time the Pussies, as they were called, were allowed to travel in the mail-coach, chaperoned by their brother Henry—a great event—was in September 1837, when they started on a round of visits in Scotland and first spent a week at Dalmeny.

Henry writes to his brother Stephen describing the beauties of Dalmeny and the extraordinary kindness of Lord[1] and Lady Rosebery:

"We found here Mr. and Mrs. Heathcote, good-natured people—he seems very uncertain in his politics, not caring to go all lengths with Lord Melbourne, yet not consenting to be a Tory. The Listers, clever and agreeable and both of them novelists. They draw and sing charmingly. Lord Bathurst on his way to Scone and Dunrobin. Music instrumental and vocal enlivens our evenings. Lady Rosebery on the harp, her son, Bouverie, on the cello, and the eldest daughter at the pianoforte. Her sister, Louisa, comes out next year and is unfortunately, at present, plain. The Scottish Service very long and dreary, one sermon following the other. The church a good specimen of Norman architecture inside and out, a rare thing in Scotland. A most lovely view of Arthur's Seat and Edinburgh Castle from the grounds; the scenery is enchanting. Mr. and Mrs. Lister draw most beautifully,

[1] Grandfather of the present Earl.

UNIV. OF
CALIFORNI

SIR STEPHEN GLYNNE
8TH BART.
From a portrait by Saunders at Hawarden Castle

and are so good-natured about giving away their drawings. We are to join the Vernons at Scone[1] on Friday. A loyal letter from Angherad Lloyd, raving of our young Queen [then just come to the throne], and hot with Conservatism. The Pussies are to travel for the first time by mail. It will be quite proper as we have taken the whole inside of the coach, and so very convenient and quick through country not specially interesting. Colonel Harcourt's marriage to Lady Catherine Jenkinson is announced—I do not envy *him*, though of course they are sure to be called the happiest of the happy.[2] The papers relate an interview between Uncle Beilby[3] and Lord Melbourne at Downing Street. Lord and Lady Rosebery are perfectly charming — it is the most delightful country house I ever was in."

When the sisters came out, they lived in their grandfather's house in Berkeley Square. Society was very exclusive in those days, and the best of it was open to them. They used to write long letters to an old Hawarden curate descriptive of their London gaieties. An account of Queen Victoria's Coronation, which they attended — with the dressing of their hair in the early morning, for they had to be in Westminster Abbey by eight; and

---

[1] The home of Lord Mansfield.
[2] Colonel Harcourt had proposed to one of the Pussies.
[3] Lord Wenlock.

again, a fancy ball at Devonshire House, to which one went as Dawn and the other as Night.

"Catherine and Mary Glynne," writes a daughter of the latter, "were but one year and a half apart in age and from their childhood, till death parted them, shared every interest, every sorrow or anxiety, and above all every joy. Married on the same day, the loving sisterly link was rather doubled than weakened, their husbands being friends before they became brothers-in-law, their children almost interchangeably beloved. The sisters were alike tall and beautiful, but in character there were many differences. Both were intense lovers of children, both had a charming gift of humour and of intuition, practically they had the same friends, men and women alike. The nature of the younger sister was more reserved, less demonstrative than Catherine, who was ever the leader; both were equally cherished and beloved. To the end they loved and influenced each other, they were one in their outlook upon life, their high moral standard, their religious principles and their deep pride in their beloved Hawarden home. Both were beautiful, noble-looking women. Mary had the more regular features, her sister more brilliant colouring."

Catherine had reigned in her beautiful home,

as Mr. Gladstone notes in his diary, a very queen. Her mother's feeling for her was little short of adoration, and with her radiant beauty and impetuosity of will she carried everything before her: her mother, her brothers, her sister, all moved as planets round the sun. It would not be easy to exchange this position of freedom and power, for the more subordinate rôle of a wife, for the duties and responsibilities of marriage and motherhood. But, as we are now to see, she fell in love.

CHAPTER II

GIRLHOOD AND MARRIAGE

IT was in November 1838 that William Gladstone, then twenty-eight years of age, met the Glynnes at Naples. Being at Christ Church with the brothers Stephen and Henry Glynne, he had already visited Hawarden Castle. He was one of a brilliant group of undergraduates — Lord Harris, the Duke of Hamilton, Canning, Lord Lincoln, afterwards Duke of Newcastle, Robin Curzon, afterwards Lord Zouche, Sir R. Phillimore, Sir Francis Doyle—who used to meet at Tabley in Cheshire, the young owner, Lord de Tabley, being also neighbour and an intimate friend of the Glynnes.

Mr. Gladstone arrived at one of the principal hotels in Naples and found it in a great commotion—" Una gran famiglia Inglese è arrivata questa sera "; Lady Glynne and her daughters and suite, as was the fashion in those days, travelling in great state in their own roomy coach, or berline as it was then called.

At Naples he dined frequently with the

Glynnes and accompanied them on their numerous expeditions, going up Mount Vesuvius with them. He left Naples (he called it "this Circean City") for Rome on December 3; the Glynnes had already gone there. Here the intercourse was more frequent, and his intimacy with the sisters grew in depth and devotion. Nearly every day they met, and he spent Christmas Day with them. There is a conversation recorded in his Diary, that took place in the gorgeous Church of Santa Maria Maggiore. They were speaking of the immense and costly amount of labour lavished on its embellishment. This led Catherine to contrasting our own parsimony in the service of God and the extravagance of our secular luxuries.

Such speculations are now constantly in the very air we breathe; but at that time, now nearly eighty years ago, they seemed little to trouble the richer classes.

"Do you think we can be justified in indulging ourselves in all these luxuries?" she said to him.

He was profoundly moved.

"I loved her for this question," he wrote in his Diary—"how sweet a thing it is to reflect that her heart and will are entirely in the hands of God. May He, in this, as in all things, be with her."

To her children, in after years, Mrs. Gladstone used to speak of the tragedy of that moonlight evening in Rome when, in spite of the glory and the romance of the circumstances and the surroundings, she failed, when they were together in the Coliseum, to respond to his first declaration of love. Yet to the brother to whom she wrote after Mr. Gladstone's return to England it must have been tolerably apparent that this condition of things could not last. Her interest in "Già," as they called him, was too deep—her constant references to him, her questions about him, her absorption in his first book on *Church and State*, of which she copied long extracts for her private use.

Here are a few passages from letters to her brother Henry, written in February 1839, he and Mr. Gladstone having left Rome for England together.

"We had so hoped to have heard from you to-day at Marseilles; we must try and be philosophic and wait patiently for another post."

She chatters of their daily doings, their gaieties, dinner parties, balls, studios—they sat to Macdonald for their busts—the numerous friends they meet, among others Lord Macaulay, above all the intercourse with Manning,[1] to her

[1] Afterwards Cardinal Archbishop of Westminster.

the most interesting and absorbing — how much, one asks, for his own sake, or how much on account of his intimacy with " Già " ?

" Write us political news, every one is so anxious here, and write soon. . . . What is the great subject of discussion in London ? Lord Glenelg's retirement from office, Già's book, or Canada ? . . . I appreciate very much the generous feelings which are expressed in his letter to me. . . . I cannot take Michael Angelo's beautiful sonnet to myself, but the sentiments contained in it are so lofty, it was impossible not to read it without the greatest delight. Please read this yourself to Già, as I particularly want the message to be given exactly. . . ." In a postscript she adds : " Tell me how you get through my message to Già and any rebound.[1] Nothing could express more honourable feelings and taste than the letter he wrote me."

Mr. Gladstone himself hardly seemed to realise any sense of assurance. He speaks in his Diary of his precipitancy, of his incorrigible stupidity and the worthlessness of his affections. In her — Catherine

---

[1] See the *Glynnese Glossary*—a volume privately printed containing a list of expressions in common use among members of the Glynne family, and employed in a sense peculiar to them. Compiled by the fourth Lord Lyttelton. Described by Mr. Gladstone as "a work of very fine scholarship." A "rebound" is "an opinion about A communicated by B to C."

Glynne — he saw what he most desired, the admiration of sacrifices made for great objects.

From the early days of April, when the Glynnes returned to their London house, 37 Berkeley Square, the intercourse was renewed —he dined with them, rode with them, met them at the breakfasts of Mr. Rogers, the poet, and at many other houses. Yet, after an hour spent with them on May 27, he wrote: " But what I ask is next to an impossibility." On June 6 he confides the state of his feelings to his father : " Concealment became too heavy for me."

All through these days his time is greatly occupied with work, in the House and in his Government Office. On June 8, at Lady Shelley's garden party at Fulham, Catherine Glynne told him that all doubts on his part might end. " I went down with the Glynnes, and here my Catherine gave me herself." They walked apart in the garden by the river, and he revealed to her his own story, and what had been the passionate desire of his heart.[1] He writes how all this produced a revulsion in her pure and lofty spirit. " She asked for the earliest Communion, that we might go together to the Altar of Christ." " May I have from my God a due sense of the

---

[1] To take Holy Orders.

value and the sweetness of this gift. Led by her questions, I have given her these passages for canons of our living :

> "Le fronde, onde s' infronda tutto l' orto
> Dell' Ortoláno Eterno, am' io cotanto,
> Quanto da Lui a lor di bene è porto." [1]

And Dante again :

> "In la sua volontade è nostro pace." [2]

Mr. Gladstone sprang from an old Scotch family, originally a race of Borderers (there is still an old Gledstanes Castle). One of his ancestors, Herbert de Gledstanes, appears in Sir Walter Scott as "gude at need." His mother was descended from Robert Bruce. It was surely a sad lack of imagination that allowed his father and grandfather to anglicise the fine name of Gledstanes into Gladstone. As a family, the brothers and sisters were tall and of a distinguished aspect. He was already a prominent member of the Conservative party, "the hope of the unbending Tories." He had been in Parliament since he was twenty-two. At the age of twenty-four (December 26, 1834), he joined the Ministry of Sir Robert Peel. It is easy to guess how the rare combination of manliness and gentleness, loftiness of

---

[1] "Love for each plant that in the garden grows
of the Eternal Gardener. I prove
Proportioned to the goodness He bestows."
"Paradiso," xxvi. 64–66.

[2] "In His Will is our peace."—"Paradiso," iii. 70.

aim and purity of mind, the powerful intellect and the pitiful heart, appealed to a girl brought up as she had been in the love and fear of God. A passage in Mr. Gladstone's Diary reads:

June 18.—" At the end of a long and chequered day—chequered with joy, business, and excitement—I sit down to write and think a little. First, how much have I thought of God to-day while my hand was coursing over the paper? How little have I thought of Him to thank Him! My blessing is indeed great. At two, she and I went to the Archbishop's [1] by his desire, and he kissed Catherine."

The following day he tells of calling with her on a tribe of her relations, including her uncle, Thomas Grenville; breakfasting with Rogers, where he met Thirlwall and Lyttelton, " in whose affairs I am deeply interested." On June 17, George Lord Lyttelton became engaged to Mary Glynne; one month earlier she had refused him. After his death a small packet was found docketed "Story of a Month." The first letter was from her brother, Sir Stephen Glynne, declining on behalf of his sister the honour of Lord Lyttelton's hand. The last was Mary's first love letter to him. So wrapped up in each other had these sisters been, so entirely content, that suitor

[1] Archbishop Harcourt.

after suitor appeared only to be rejected; it was possibly the coincidence of two of the most brilliant men of their day, in character, the most lofty and pure, happening to fall in love with them at the same time that brought about the miracle.

Mrs. Gladstone told one of her nieces, in later years, how George (Lord Lyttelton), in a tempest of uncontrollable joy, rushed down the stairs into the room below, where Mr. Gladstone and Catherine were anxiously awaiting developments.

In Mr. Gladstone's Diary. "Mary was much overcome, and hid her face in Catherine's bosom; then they fled away 'for a little." Mr. Gladstone drew Lord Lyttelton on to his knees. "For a while he could not control his emotions, and yet he directed them towards God. He is a very noble and powerful creature."

"He was a man of rare attainments: a beautiful scholar, his nature full of sharp contrasts — vigorous, tempestuous, devout, tender."

They met daily, riding, walking, driving. "Sent off a snowstorm of excuses for all pending parties." Then came a flight to Eton—the two pairs of lovers—for Sunday.

"There is no end to our subjects—or to our interruptions," he says. It is easy to imagine what a bower of love and ecstasy the Berkeley Square house must have become in those summer months, with the two radiant pairs of lovers.

"Time flies, and yet in retrospect we seem to have lived through months." "Nuptial shopping." "All joy broken into shivers by constant interruption. I suppose the craving for something like continuance of repose by her side is the disease of self-love. We had been very anxious to be married by banns, but are reluctantly compelled to give it up—it is not a matter on which shocking people is worth while. . . . Routing out and struggling to arrange papers for C. . . . Come semplice di trovar solo un cotal diffetto."

One of Catherine's dearest friends, Lady Brabazon, wrote to wish her joy of marrying one who would now help her to write and answer her letters !

And here, with his orderly habits, he must have felt some dismay. She often, in after life, used to tease him—" What a bore you would have been, if you had married somebody as tidy as you."

July 8. — "Assisting in Catherine's and Mary's arrangement of books, etc., they have lived with community of goods—beautiful—settling papers, letters, etc., most joyously for departure."

Hawarden Castle.

UNIV. OF
CALIFORNIA

Contrary to modern custom, three weeks before the wedding, the bridegrooms seem to have gone down to Hawarden, then in perfection of summer beauty, with Lady Glynne and her daughters, there to spend what must have been a heavenly time. Riding, driving, strolling, sitting out in the evening, visiting their friends, the schools, reading aloud.

When Mr. Gladstone and Lord Lyttelton arrived at Hawarden, as they walked together down the village street—the one tall and upright, pale, resolute, with eyes like an eagle; the other, spite of massive head and intellectual brow, somewhat rugged and uncouth in manner and appearance—he was only twenty-one—it was said by a passer-by, gazing with admiration on Mr. Gladstone: " Isn't it easy to see which is the lord ? "

" *Kenilworth* aloud with dearest,"—" much real intercourse. What am I, to charge myself with the care of such a being, and to mingle her destiny with mine ? Instruction and profit on this earth do not usually come on the wings of joy so unmixed."

July 21. — " Special Communion. George, Mary, Catherine and I—Henry much affected —many arrangements about rejoicings, fireworks, festivities for children and old people. The Nevilles arrived. Jane Lawley and Helen assisting Catherine and Mary in warmly greeting the old people."

The eve of the wedding, settlements and pecuniary matters occupied the time, but at midnight the lovers walked in the garden— "a fine night—we spoke together of our great felicity."

On July 25, the wedding day, he speaks of his "too sound slumbers having been broken"—"Rose in good time and read the Psalms." Soon after ten, Sir Watkin Wynn having arrived, they set off from the Castle in twelve carriages, starting by the park, over the grass below the old castle, along the moat, into and through the village. "Oh, what a scene—such an outpouring of pure human affection on these beloved girls, combined with so solemn a mystery!" He describes every house a bower, the road arched and festooned with flowers, the deepest interest in every face—bands, processions of societies, the crowd thickening as they approached the church, the road carpeted, the churchyard path strewn with flowers by the hands of children. He speaks of the music breaking down what little self-control he had left, as he walked up the crowded church with Lord Lyttelton. At the altar he found his beloved, and they were married first— the same opening and conclusion for both.

"Uncle George[1] performed the service with dignity and great feeling, and entire [*i.e.* no omissions]. My beloved bore up. Her soul is as high and strong as it is tender." "Lord Lyttelton broke down, and in all the rejoicing there were many inevitable tears."

The sisters changed their bridal attire at the Rectory, the Lytteltons honeymooning at Hagley, the Gladstones at Norton Priory in Cheshire, the home of their dearest friends the Brookes.

At 5 p.m. of the same afternoon, he writes his journal while "the beloved sleeps on the sofa. We have read the lessons together. She sleeps gently as a babe—oh, may I never disturb her precious peace!"

On July 26 they read the Bible together: "The daily practice will, I trust, last as long as our joint lives."

On that day, looking back at the Hawarden wedding :—

"How can I express," he writes, "the sense of the scene yesterday—it may seem extravagant to dwell so much on the accompaniments, but it is because they did ennoble and sanctify the scene and did really, for the time, raise the heart to a high level according with the spirit of the great mystery of Christian marriage." And on a later day : "Not only

[1] Dean of Windsor.

every day, but nearly every hour, convince me of the brightness of my treasure, her pure enduring brightness."

Subjects of conversation and discussion are mentioned—on amusements, on the fallacy of private judgments, on the Lord's Day and how it should be kept, on charity and expenditure, on the sanctity of time as a trust committed to us, on the responsibilities of money. There was much that she had to learn from him, much that the engagement had not shown her. She used to tell us, long afterwards, that it was something of a shock to both sisters when, after marriage, any little waiting time, as at the railway station, which during their engagement would have been spent in love-making, was now spent in reading —both husbands carrying the inevitable little classic in their pockets. Out it would come and quickly engross the owner. Lord Lyttelton was to be seen at cricket matches in the playing field at Eton, lying on his front, reading between the overs, but never missing a ball.

It was a blissful honeymoon, though must she not have felt that it bordered on austerity— his stern habits of self-control?

They called on the clergyman to arrange their gifts in charity.

The four met again at Hawarden in August:

" A beautiful meeting between the sisters—

Lady Glynne still depending as much as ever on Catherine. A servants' ball that night."

Sir Francis Doyle, Professor of Poetry at Oxford, was at Hawarden for the wedding, evidently playing the part of best man to one of the two bridegrooms. He was one of the illustrious group of Mr. Gladstone's contemporaries, most of whom played a distinguished part in after life. He gave expression to his thoughts in a poem dedicated " To Two Sister Brides " (now published in his collected works). The following extracts foreshadow something of the part played by the elder sister in after life:

> "High hopes are thine, O eldest flower,
>   Great duties to be greatly done,
> To soothe in many a toil-worn hour
>   The noble heart that thou hast won.
>
> Covet not then the rest of those
>   Who sleep through life unknown to fame;
> Fate grants not passionless repose
>   To her who weds a glorious name.
>
> He presses on through calm and storm
>   Unshaken, let what will betide ;
> Thou hast an office to perform,
>   To be his answering spirit bride.
>
> The path appointed for his feet
>   Through desert wilds and rocks may go,
> Where the eye looks in vain to greet
>   The gales that from the waters blow.
>
> Be thou a balmy breeze to him,
>   A fountain singing at his side,
> A star whose light is never dim,
>   A pillar to uphold and guide."

On August 18 the two bridal pairs set forth, with their respective carriages, by sea to Greenock, and from there they drove, day by day, through glorious scenery—Loch Katrine and the Trossachs, Glencoe, Inveraray, Dunkeld, Taymouth ("magnificent in natural features, the house would be fine but for the surpassing grandeur around"), Aberfeldy, Blairgowrie to Fasque.

One can hardly conceive a honeymoon so delightfully and unusually spent, the sisters meeting daily for meals and at night for rest at the inns, comparing notes. Sometimes walking, sometimes riding or driving.

In a biography is written the following description taken from the diary of Henry Reeve [1]:

"Walking through the wild passes from Loch Katrine to Inversnaid, two couples in the party excited our attention. Both handsome, and dressed alike in the Lennox plaid. The sister brides were mounted on Highland ponies, each one attended by her most faithful and attentive squire, holding her bridle over the gullies and burns. We guessed they were brides, and at last Charles Hamilton made a brilliant shot, and we recognised them as the two sisters who were married the other

---

[1] Henry Reeve, once Editor of the *Edinburgh Review*.

FASQUE
THE HOME OF SIR JOHN GLADSTONE, BART.

[D. Ross

day at Hawarden, on the same day, to William Gladstone and Lord Lyttelton. A prettier, happier party never crossed the heather."

After a fortnight at Fasque, their brother Stephen having joined them, they posted to Ballater and Braemar, in ecstasy over the Deeside scenery, scaling Lochnagar, " and we fare sumptuously every day."

Many reflections in his Diary and stern resolutions scrupulously kept. The Gladstones returned to Fasque in September, and on the 23rd Catherine wrote to Mary, telling her how she had revealed her secret to her husband:

" I imagine you receiving this at Chatsworth, dressed very smart and sitting in a fine dressing-room, unless in one of the grand rooms below. Poor little thing, you will feel shy, I know. I shall long for your letter." Both sisters had the happiest anticipations for the summer of 1840, and the time had come when their hopes might be shared. . In a passage of infinite tenderness and beauty, but too sacred for quotation, Mrs. Gladstone describes to this sister of her heart, in what way he guessed the happy secret—the old, old secret, yet ever new; his whispered benediction, and then the long silence, too deep for words, as he held her close to his heart.

Lass der feuchten Perlen ungewohnte Zier
Freudig hell erzittern in dem Auge mir.
Wusst ich nur mit Worten, wie ich's sagen soll ;
Komm und birg dein Antlitz hier an meiner Brust,
Will in's Ohr dir flüstern alle meine Lust.
Bleib' an meinem Herzen, fühle dessen Schlag.
Dass ich fest und fester nur dich drücken mag,
Fest und fester !
Hier, an meinem Bette hat die Wiege Raum,
Wo—sie still verberge meinem holden Traum ;
Kommen wird der Morgen, wo der Traum erwacht,
Und daraus, dein Bildnis mir entgegen lacht—
Dein Bildnis.[1]

And another day she says to her sister, from Hawarden, in the following year : " My dearest, I found your letter upon arriving here very refreshing, for the getting home renews our separation. It was blue to be without you, specially here. How disturbed we used to be when one of us was out of the room for any little time even : it is not to be wondered at now, when miles and miles have parted us and you can no longer enter the room."

The list of books mentioned as read during the honeymoon and its continuation at Fasque :—

Scott, Trench, Keble, Lyttelton's *Dialogues*, Bishop of London on Education, Hope, Hallam, Dickens (finished *Nicholas Nickelby*: " It's

---

[1] Words immortalised by Schumann for all lovers: "She knows not how to break to him her secret ? In her eyes the happy tears glisten. If she can only find words—heart close to heart, she will whisper to him all her trembling rapture. .... A cradle will hold her dream—and the morning and the dream-child will awaken, and reveal to her the image of her beloved."

length will, I fear, sink it—the tone very human—he is most happy in touches of natural pathos—the motives in the book are not those of religion"). Rothe's *Aufunge der Christlichen Kirche* is one of the books studied, but surely not by her! Mr. Gladstone's copy, now at St. Deiniol's Library at Hawarden, bears signs of most serious reading, copiously marked, during the honeymoon. The books strike one as being rather severe. But there seems to have been plenty of diversion; the two delighted in billiards and chess. In the latter Mrs. Gladstone must have shown no little skill. The tradition survives that Mr. Gladstone beat Mrs. Gladstone, that Mrs. Gladstone beat Lord Lyttelton, and that Lord Lyttelton beat Mr. Gladstone. In the autumn of his marriage year he remarks: " C. and I in deadly conflict—too great an expenditure, perhaps, of thought and interest"—and this was chess!

They remained at Fasque for two months, then posted through Scotland and England, visiting various country houses, among them Escrich, the home of her uncle and aunt, "where C. is loved as a child," reaching Hawarden on Christmas Eve, where they find the Lytteltons. The Brabazons were of the party. In the Diary he descibes this greatest friend of his wife[1]:

[1] Lady Brabazon was daughter of Sir R. Brooke.

"A discussion with Lady Brabazon on Ireland and the Irish Church—the prettiest sight possible—she is so ingenuous, sincere, acute, earnest, playful, and inconsistent, her propositions being founded on single and reciprocally contradictory instincts, never compared and reviewed by the understanding. In short, most characteristically feminine."

Their first parting was January 12, 1840, she going to Hagley.

"Left my own at Wolverhampton—a week's parting stings."

But he joined her at Hagley on January 22, and together they went to London, living in his father's house in Carlton Gardens until the house Mr. Gladstone had bought was furnished and ready. The first starting of their London home, 13 Carlton House Terrace, was a great event; it was undertaken by both in a spirit of the utmost seriousness and sense of responsibility: "Except the Lord build the house: their labour is but lost that build it."

The house was large and grand for a couple unencumbered by children, but Lady Glynne had her rooms there while in London, and the Lytteltons always found a home and a welcome. Much pains were taken in the preparation of household rules and regulations. Daily Family Prayers, and on Sundays he wrote a short Address for Evening Prayers. He taught in the Sunday School at Bedfordbury, Chapel of Ease to St. Martin's in the Fields, and so great was their sense of parochial duty that there was a yearly school feast on the terrace besides constant visiting in the parish.

The Lytteltons first came to stay on March 26, 1840. Both the sisters had happy hopes for the following summer. On April 28, the first book-case was put up. In speaking gravely of buying " material things," Mr. Gladstone notes that " Beauty is beauty even in furniture." They arranged a servants' library with great thought and care, and in all things their aims were for the good of others.

They entertained largely, and very soon started the Thursday ten o'clock breakfasts which were so interesting a feature in their lives. They were greatly sought after, and entered into the social entertainments of the day, visiting (often accompanied by a baby in arms) the stately homes of their friends.

CHAPTER III

EARLY DIARIES AND MARRIED LIFE

MRS. GLADSTONE was no expert in diary jottings, and the few that remain show signs of having been undertaken from a sense of duty, certainly not from a sense of pleasure—unlike her letters, they are not quite alive. To people like her the stimulus, the inspiration of letter-writing lies in the knowledge that they are written to and for one particular person—in a diary there is no direct sense of intercourse, and the lack of an audience becomes to some as deadening as talking in an empty room. Here and there we come across an interesting note, but on the whole the diaries give little impression of the brilliant social and political circle in which the young husband and wife lived.

It was early in 1840 that the first entries were made—dinners with the Archbishop of York (Harcourt) to meet Queen Adelaide, the Duke and Duchess of Cambridge, etc. At Mr. Hallam's she sits next to Guizot, who speaks English to her, Mr. and Mrs. Grote, the Hawtreys. Quizzical remarks on the appearance of Mrs. Grote and on the manner in which Marie, Marchioness of Ailesbury, dresses her hair.

She never goes to a party at Buckingham Palace without an expression of special appreciation of the girl Queen's grace and dignity. Her Majesty was only twenty, and some awkwardness and shyness would only have been natural. Her marriage with the Prince Consort took place a few months after the double wedding at Hawarden, and this fact made a special link between Her Majesty and the sister brides. In the years that followed there was constant comparing of notes as to their respective children, as will be recorded later on. Her first meeting with the Duke of Wellington was at the Duke of Northumberland's house: "He went out of his way to speak to William—very interesting to watch the people's manners with him."

In June of that year the first boy was born. To the parents the ever new miracle of life causes them to regard this event as quite out of the common, and to consider that the baby is as different as possible from all other babies. His mother says of his christening at St. Martin's, "He never cried through the whole Morning Service, and the manner in which he threw out his arms as Henry received him was quite overpowering. Godfathers and godmother: Mr. Hope, Mr. Manning, and Mary" (Lady Lyttelton). Meriel Lyttelton was born a fortnight later.

The following year Mrs. Gladstone had the delight of sitting next the Iron Duke at the house of the Archbishop of York. "I was pleased to think he had spoken to me before either of us died—I have long wished for this." In April 1841 she mentions first meeting the Prime Minister. This was at the house of Lady Jersey, whose son, Lord Villiers, was just engaged to the daughter of Sir Robert Peel. Mrs. Gladstone was deeply flattered to find that the great man had asked to be introduced to her.

In September 1841, she was present at the Consecration of Bishop Selwyn—"That fine, touching service, never to be heard without emotion, but in the present instance how peculiarly affecting! He was leaving his native land and all that he held most dear. . . . We visited the Bishop at his house at Eton so as to be present at the dinner given by Mr. Coleridge the day before the farewell sermon at Windsor. There were forty present. I sat between Judge Patterson and Dr. Hawtrey, the Head Master. Mr. Coleridge proposed the health of the Bishop in a touching speech, for which the Bishop returned thanks. Devoted to the service of God, he is able to feel the step

Mrs. Gladstone and her Sister, Lady Lyttelton, on the Lawn at Hawarden

he has taken not as a sacrifice but as a privilege : he unites unusual tenderness of feeling to great manliness of character. The scene was an extraordinary one. Casting the eye down a long table, most of the guests were in tears, men and women sobbing, and poor old Dr. Keate[1] (to-day was my first introduction to him), his head bowed down upon the table, his face buried in his handkerchief. I never witnessed such devotion. The farewell sermon at Windsor was striking and affecting : ' Thou hast set my feet in a large room.' A crowded congregation, not even standing room."—" Evidently he is not allowing himself to think of returning to live in England. Very touching was the way he spoke to me of his wife : ' She feels just as I could wish— all the tenderness of a woman joined to the greatest resolution.' "

London is evidently lonely to her with her husband's long hours of official work (he was then Vice-President of the Board of Trade and Master of the Mint). " I am greatly relieved to be with him, but he works hard all the time he is at home and it is a little dreary sometimes." No wonder, when one remembers that in office it was habitual with him to work fourteen hours a day. " I have been reading Hook's *Sermons*, and Warren's

[1] Late Head Master of Eton, 1809-34.

Ten Thousand a Year: the latter, although vulgar, is clever and interesting."

January 6, 1842.—" I am thirty to-day— terrible thought! We had a dinner party for Uncle Tom.[1] He sat an hour with me in the afternoon—as he walked from Hamilton Place and back, this was pretty well for eighty-seven." She mentions a City dinner to meet the Prince Consort: " Peel spoke well, and the Prince was evidently affected by his allusion to the dear ties which bound him (the Prince) to England. Elizabeth Fry sat between the Prince and the Prime Minister."

That month she mentions in her Diary how at Hagley " Willy and Meriel, at a year and a half, play very prettily together. Both kneel down when told and put their hands together and say, ' Papa, Mama, Amen.' Meriel the merriest. He obstreperous and a complete boy—I like to feel they have been taught to kneel and put their hands together before they could speak, and anticipate great delight when their little minds go with their outward actions."

" I am looking after Lady de Tabley—the more I see of her the more I like her—no one can properly appreciate her who does not know her well—such purity and goodness with

---

[1] Right Hon. T. Grenville. He bequeathed his famous library at Dropmore to the British Museum.

great unselfishness of disposition and devoted to her husband and children."

They spent a week at Magdalene College at Cambridge, and she is struck by the great honour paid to her husband, the intense interest taken in him.

January 20, 1842.—" William met the King of Prussia [1] at Bunsen's. H.M. was full of his book [*Church and State*]. Lady Canning the only lady except the hostess. A queer medley—clergy, Quakers, scientists, and politicians. I was dining with Mrs. Grenville, meeting the Duchess of Sutherland,[2] Lord and Lady Mahon, Mr. Harcourt, Mr. Samuel Rogers. I was pleased with the Duke and Duchess—she spoke nicely and naturally about nursing her babies."

She attends parties at Stafford House and Apsley House, given in honour of the King. "The Duke of Wellington sat close to the pianoforte listening to the music, apparently lost to everything besides." She sits next Lord Stanley (afterwards Prime Minister) and revels in his wit: " At all events, he can shake off the cares of office."

The Prime Minister had made an offer to Mr. Gladstone, February 1842, which had as usual been confided to her.

---

[1] Frederick William IV.
[2] Afterwards their dearest friend.

February 7.—" I in my turn had to tell something to William to-day. He is in great spirits, and what joy did it not give me when he told me I had been of some use to him the day before. In the midst of such toil as his it is often a grief to me how little real assistance I can be to him."

February 13.—" A note from Sir Robert Peel desiring William to follow Lord John Russell in the House on Monday, on the Corn Laws. He made no preparation to-day."

February 14.—" This has been a happy chance which fixed my night at the House of Commons for his speech. I found myself nearly upon Lady John Russell's lap, with Lady Palmerston and other wives near. Funny, we began talking, though before unacquainted, and I told her my husband was to answer hers, which news she received with the greatest interest; she said her heart was beating, and she was all attention when Lord John began. He spoke for an hour and a half with eloquence and cleverness. It was quite pain to me before William rose, but before he had said many words there was something at once so spirited and so collected in his manner that all fright was lost in intense interest and delight. Pride is perhaps not the right feeling—great thankfulness was mixed up with it. We heard him very well—

he was rapid and without the smallest hesitation throughout. Peel was evidently delighted, and from all I gather this speech has made a great sensation. We had coffee in our room afterwards—how snug I need hardly describe—indeed I could not."

This was Mr. Gladstone's first great speech on the Corn Laws, a landmark in their lives, as it was in history, signifying his first fundamental divergence with protection.

The Bill he was defending, introduced by the Prime Minister for lessening the duty on corn, was really what Lord Morley calls "the first invasion of the old Tory Corn Law of 1827."

The epoch was, in Mr. Gladstone's own words, "an agitated and expectant age." He had inherited the system of protection almost as he had inherited his religion, but as he reached manhood it was qualified by his belief in Mr. Huskisson. In 1833, a speech against the Corn Laws had made him feel uncomfortable. In 1841, his mind was "a sheet of white paper." But as Vice-President of the Board of Trade he worked hard, and every day so spent "beat like a battering-ram on the unsure fabric of my official protectionism. By the end of that year I was far gone in the opposite sense." He was wrestling with the difficulties of two opposed systems. Into the intricacies of the measures proposed by Sir

Robert Peel for the modification of the Corn Laws there is no need to enter. As a subordinate though always influential member of the Government, Mr. Gladstone's mind worked ahead of the plans of his chief. With further authority, after his appointment in 1842 as President of the Board of Trade, he passed from a sliding scale and its " vicious operation " on the corn trade to his great work of tariff revision, the removal of hundreds of restrictions, and the practical acceptance of the principles of Mr. Cobden. In the course of six years he freed three hundred and seventy-one commodities from taxation; thus he put it into the power of the people to buy food and many other necessities that, up till then, had been practically out of their reach.

February 15.—" Sir T. Fremantle and Mr. G. Hope we met in our early walk. They praised the speech and told me how every one was talking of it. William's father nearly upset me in his enthusiasm, his eyes filling with tears."

February 16.—" William is so modest about his speech, and yet he literally cannot escape the knowledge of his success. He turns the subject by saying, 'It is better not to speak of it.'

" Many congratulations."

February 20.—" I have had very little of

William this week, and have felt unduly vexed. I fear he must get ill from this excessive labour. We went to church together on Wednesday. I have great comfort in my darling boy—I cannot be too thankful."

Her life is very full of social engagements, and she met and conversed with many interesting people—Sidney Smith, Wordsworth, Macaulay, Moore, etc. She occasionally dined out alone—"which I detest." She records a talk with Lord Mahon [1] regarding her husband, "his manner is so straightforward and his arguments convincing." Among other things Lord Ripon prophesied to her, "I see clearly his destination, but the first step—he will be Chancellor of the Exchequer." She delighted in Lord Stanley, losing her awe of him. They compared notes as to official life, and Lord Stanley told her how, late at night, with his feet in hot water, he partook of the most gossamer meal; subsequently reading a novel to compose himself to sleep. When Chief Secretary for Ireland, he told her, he worked eighteen hours a day—he maintained that with strenuous mental work there is no need for bodily exercise. He prided himself on twenty years' experience. He took off various tricks in speakers of note, specially Peel, who, he declared, was often exceedingly

[1] Afterwards Lord Stanhope.

nervous. He told anecdotes so well—one of a dinner at Peel's, when a boring man sitting next the Duke of Wellington regaled him with long trolls[1] on India. The Duke sat silent, his chin on his chest, with an occasional grunt; the bore went on and on, till the Duke remarked quietly in a pause, "I have been in India."

She describes a fancy dress ball at the Palace, where "Mary went as Henrietta Maria, and I as Claude, wife of Francis i.—deep crimson petticoat and cap, large flowing sleeves of tissue. The sight very striking—specially the royal procession."

Putney was deep in the country at that time, and they much enjoyed going out to Ripon House for dinner. Lord and Lady Ripon liked her to come, when tired or delicate, for change of air.

In July 1842, she records how glad she was to be handed in by the Prime Minister and that she could tell him herself how deeply she had been touched by the words he had written about Mr. Gladstone.

"At no time," he wrote in June 1842, "in the annals of Parliament has there been exhibited a more admirable combination of ability, extensive knowledge, temper, and discretion—your feelings must be gratified in the highest degree by the success which has

[1] Meaning rigmarole; see *Glynnese Glossary*.

naturally and justly followed his intellectual exertions; and that the capacity to make such exertions is combined, in his case, with such purity of heart and integrity of spirit."

Sir Robert Peel told her he had read a letter from the Duke of Wellington soon after he entered the Army, in which he expresses an earnest hope that he may be able to resign his Commission " as there seemed no chance of any promotion for him." Had his prayer been granted, the course of history might indeed have been changed! Peel had been shown a most touching letter to the Queen, from the King of France,[1] on the death of his son.

" Peel told me he required very little sleep, and could get but little rest when his mind was occupied. He regretted the amount of political power which the Duke of Wellington still had."

She describes the Princess Royal[2] as a very interesting child, the image of the Queen. "I played on the pianoforte, which delighted her. She tried to dance, and when I stopped called for 'more' [she was then twenty months old]. The Prince of Wales a fine, fair, satisfactory baby, upon whom William and I gazed with deep interest. . We kissed his little hand. Who could look at him and think of his destiny

[1] Louis Philippe.
[2] Afterwards Crown Princess of Germany and Empress.

without emotion!" This recalls the occasion, fifty years later, when Mr. and Mrs. Gladstone at St. James's Palace paid their respects to the little Prince David (now Prince of Wales), then one year old.

In September 1842, Mr. Gladstone, while out shooting at Hawarden, had a narrow escape. His gun went off as he was muzzle-loading, blowing away the first finger of the left hand.

"What a day I might have to record!" she writes in her Diary. "God has been merciful to me; may the memory of it sink into my heart, and the rest of my days prove my gratitude. I drove to meet the shooting party in the Irish car. I met Henry. His pale face aroused my fears. 'What has happened to William?' How can I express what I felt before he could answer. Oh, gracious God, was all earthly happiness to be dashed away? I found my precious one at the Rectory, calm and cheerful, only thinking of his escape and how to make the best of it for me. It was then three, and the accident had happened at two. The whole time before the operation, and even while it was going on, never did one word of complaint pass his lips—patient, brave, gentle, and even cheerful." Two operations proved to be necessary, as the surgeon first used the knife in the wrong place; and if the absence of all anæsthetics is remembered, the agony of pain which Mr. Gladstone suffered with absolute serenity testified to his self-control. "I sat in the next room" (she was not allowed to be with him, as her confinement was to take place in October) "till Mr. Phillimore came. He was overcome by his emotion, and burst into tears; the extraordinary courage shown by William would be a lesson to him, he said, through life. He had held the patient's hand throughout the operations. Little time was lost in moving him to the Castle, and he was given a composing draught for the night. How sweet was the consciousness to me of his quiet breathing as I watched him while he slept!"

They were able to get to London on the tenth day, and for another fortnight they led as quiet a life as was possible under the circumstances. "The poor hand goes on well, there are no untoward symptoms, no fever or swelling, and oh, the difference in the dressing of the wound and the bandages! Scott does all he can to build up his strength. We play at chess most nights; and are very snug and quiet."

October 18. — "Drove in the Park with William. My little girl was born at 8 p.m., a fine healthy baby with pretty features."

The babies, from the scanty records in her Diary, seemed to arrive very casually and made little interruption in the social life. But there is a separate record of the children, in a book full of delicious notes and descriptions, hardly suitable for quotation, but revealing the beautiful mother-love and the utmost watchfulness and devoted care. Nothing seemed to escape her vigilant eye in their comings and their goings, in their characteristics, all the little ailments and their treatment, the little sayings and doings. No tiniest seed of character passed unheeded. During the first thirteen and a half years of marriage eight children were born to Mr. and Mrs. Gladstone, and ten during the same period to Lord and Lady Lyttelton, so, as it will readily be believed, there was frequent comparing of notes between the sisters. When apart, they wrote daily to one another; together, they still passed a great deal of their time in the capacious London house in Carlton House Terrace, with many weeks spent by the Lytteltons at Hawarden or the Gladstones at Hagley. There was still much community of goods between the Pussies—interchange of servants, clothes, even furniture, etc. In 1847, there were eleven children in the house under seven—six Lytteltons and five Gladstones. One can scarcely imagine how anyone could safely cross the room with such a crowd about the floor.

In the inimitable *Glynnese Glossary* Lord Lyttelton wrote a few years later: "On entering a room at Hagley or Hawarden during one of those great confluences of families which occur among the Glynnese, and finding seventeen children upon the floor under the age of twelve, and consequently all inkstands, books, carpets, furniture, ornaments, in intimate intermixture and in every form of fraction and confusion," etc.

In these luxurious days of rapid motion, of trains and motors instead of the stage coach, the private travelling carriage, or the creeping trains of those days, one reflects with astonishment, almost with incredulity, on these vast pilgrimages, with their avalanches of mothers and nurses and little ones, from Hawarden to Hagley or London, or *vice versa*. In June 1843: "Left Hawarden, seventeen of us without counting the children." "Lytteltons went away, eighteen souls in all." So we read in Mrs. Gladstone's letters or Diary.

"Weighed the babies, Agnes and Charles; she is 14 lb., he is 14·7. Most people are struck by her beauty—the eyes peculiarly fine and very expressive, dark blue in colour, the sweetest thing that ever was. She takes great notice [six weeks old], laughs at her father's whistling most prettily."

January 6, 1843.—" William to London—these partings do not get any easier."

To the Ladies' Gallery she was already a frequent visitor, and records the most notable speeches. Lord Stanley's in the Irish debate. One night she heard Sheil, the Irish orator: " His style was fluent and his speech brilliant, but ranting, and the voice peculiarly discordant and unpleasing." Lord Ashley [1] on the White Slave Trade in the factories.[2] She mentions Cardwell and Buller as two of the best speakers. She listened for the first time to a speech of the Duke of Wellington in the House of Lords (7th March 1843), and also mentions hearing Lord Lyndhurst and Lord Brougham.

But she keeps all her most enthusiastic admiration for her husband's speeches.

Much later a note occurs in the *Recollections of an Irish Judge* testifying to her constant presence in the Ladies' Gallery:

" In the House one day I noticed, looking at the Ladies' Gallery, that a small patch of the dull brass grille shone like burnished gold. I asked an attendant if he could explain it. ' That,' said he, ' is the place where Mrs. Gladstone sits to watch the Grand Old Man whenever he speaks—she rests one hand on the grating, and the friction, as you see, has

---

[1] Afterwards Lord Shaftesbury.   [2] Factory Bill.

worn it bright.' Often afterwards I watched the eager face close to the grille, with one hand resting lightly on the grating." [1]

Their life, as judged from the diaries and letters of the day, in spite of the immense number of entertainments given or attended by them, still strikes one as singularly serious and strenuous—they seemed to enter no part of life light-heartedly.

It is impossible not to smile over the following quite serious entry: "Engaged a cook; after a long conversation on *religious matters, chiefly between her and William.*"

Apparently he shared very much more in those days in the domestic machinery than has been commonly thought—long grave talks with any erring servant or any of the weaker brethren. There are pages and pages of his letters at this date concerning an ass travelling with them as personal luggage, the doctors having ordered asses' milk for the reigning baby.

"A dinner at Mr. Samuel Rogers', more than ordinarily clerical in character: the Archbishop of Canterbury, the Bishop of London and Mrs. Blomfield, Wordsworth and Tommy Moore, etc. Mr. R. whispered to me that he was much oppressed at having the heads of the Church to dine with him. I never saw him so little at ease."

[1] *Recollections of an Irish Judge*, by M. McD. Bodkin.

March 17.—" We dined at the Palace. Clanwilliams, Lord Rosebery, Lord Palmerston, Lord Sydney, who took me in. After dinner the Queen asked me to tell her about William's accident, and questioned me as to the children and Mary. She has more expression when speaking than I thought [she was twenty-three at the time]. Really enjoyed my evening; was surprised at its being so little formal. Boy [1] is sitting to Mr. Richmond, who finds him difficult."

There is great sorrow over the guilt of a housemaid, taken up for stealing, and she describes minutely what she went through, for she had to give evidence at Bow Street against the poor girl: " She pleaded guilty, and William, in a short speech, recommended her to mercy. He was affected, and so was I." They visited her afterwards in prison and at the penitentiary.

In May 1843, the Prime Minister offered her husband a seat in the Cabinet as President of the Board of Trade. The whole crux lay in Church questions; both Manning and Hope were consulted:

" I walked with him in Kensington Gardens. He was much oppressed—the great anxiety to act rightly. He asked me to pray for him. How thankful I am to be joined to one whose

[1] William Henry, born June 1840.

mind is purity and integrity itself! If I have received joy and pride in Peel's letter to him, how much more do I feel in seeing the way he received the offer, in witnessing the tenderness of conscience which shrinks from any idea of worldly gain lest it should conflict with higher duties!"

May 15.—" Manning and Hope advised his going direct to Peel to set forth clearly his position. He has accepted. God bless and prosper him—may the increase of responsibility not injure his precious health. How I wish he could have a horse!"

At the end of July 1843, she went to Hawarden with her sister and their children, for the consecration of the new church Sir Stephen Glynne had built in the parish. Dr. Hook was the preacher and deeply impressed them all—" such warmth and simplicity, his heart overflowing with goodness." There is great joy over the engagement of Henry Glynne, her brother, and Lavinia Lyttelton, then staying at the Castle. This made a double link with Hagley. "The two—Henry Glynne and Lavinia Lyttelton—walked together in the garden. He gave her a rose. There was no need for any words. She understood. She afterwards placed the rose within the leaves of her Prayer Book." Nearly a century has passed away; the rose, faintly coloured, still lies in the book, treasured by her surviving daughter.[1] "Oh, what joy and thanksgiving throughout the house!—even little Willy and Meriel partaking of the unmixed happiness, though unconscious of its real meaning [they were only just three years old]. . . . 'Aunt Lavinia is to marry Uncle Henry,' their dear voices announcing the tidings to the wondering nurses."

In October, after seven weeks at Fasque, they travelled outside the mail-coach in very turbulent weather. Leaving Perth at midnight, they crossed the water at Queensferry about 4 a.m., and travelled the two following days, reaching London in the evening.

The wedding took place at St. George's, October 1848. "Henry breakfasting with us, much affected at first seeing me. Never did I see her look so beautiful as she stood at the altar. How blessed to feel such confidence in their happiness, a happiness built on duty! I imagine their life hand in hand, spurring one another to good and holy acts—a labour of love.' But their wedded life was to be brief and clouded. Five children were born; one of them, the much-wished-for son and heir, died while the joy-bells were ringing for his birth. In 1850, the lovely mother passed away, one

[1] Gertrude, Lady Penrhyn.

fortnight after giving birth to her youngest daughter. The Dowager Lady Lyttelton gave up her Court appointment so as to have more time to spend at Hawarden Rectory with the motherless little ones.

November 3.—" In London again. A most interesting evening. Archdeacon Manning slept here." They talked till midnight. Dinners with the Duke of Wellington, with the Cannings, with the Duke and Duchess of Buccleuch. She comments on the deep interest manifested by the Duke, when she sat next him, in the great contrasts of life— in the poverty and misery to be found in London side by side with great affluence.

From one of the Ancient Concerts, she mentions with pride her being handed out by the Duke of Wellington. "He insisted on escorting us down the long room to our carriage. I was fearful lest he should catch cold in the draught. He merely placed his cocked hat upon his head. How characteristic, in all he says and does, is the honesty and peculiar straightforwardness of his character!"

Then come notes on the Duc and Duchesse de Nemours, and on Nicholas, the Emperor of Russia, whom they met at the Palace:

"A noble-looking personage, the figure so striking, tall, and commanding, his manners civil and courteous, friendly without losing his dignity. The form and manner struck me more than the face itself, yet there is something peculiarly awful in the eyes which seem to look straight through one—it was interesting to watch him and the Duke of Wellington together. The manner in which the Queen took his arm, and his in giving it to her, was striking and graceful—the great inequality of their heights would never have been suspected, such was the grace and ease with which they walked off together."

The Dowager Lady Lyttelton told her how much impressed the Emperor was by the footing between the Royal children and their parents:

S. L.—" How happy it is that the Queen and Prince have succeeded in keeping their domestic relations like those of a private family, and can feel real family happiness and comfort! C'est là, Sire, le vrai bonheur de la vie."

Emperor.—" Le vrai bonheur ? *Le seul bonheur pour nous autres.*"

S. L.—" Non, Sire, pas le seul."

Emperor.—" Ah, Madame, nous n'en avons guère d'autre. C'est un dur métier que le nôtre."

Sir Robert Peel spoke to her most feelingly

of the beautiful happiness of the domestic life of the Queen and the Prince Consort. Brougham was close by, and she delighted in listening to the talk between him and Peel.

"At three and a half Willy is making some little progress in reading and can manage a sentence composed of words of two or three letters. I only give him ten minutes a day. He likes the Sunday lesson given him by his father, and reflects as he lies in his little bed. One night he told us he had been 'talking to God.' 'What did you say, Willy?'—'I said, "Listen to me."' After the joy of his birthday party they found him crying when they visited him in bed. 'I feel ungoodly,' he said."

In the following words Mrs. Gladstone describes the emotion of his friends and colleagues when her husband, early in 1845, resigned on the Maynooth Grant. Only a few years had elapsed since he had published his treatise on *The Church in its Relation to the State*. Though his mind, slowly but surely, had reached a more comprehensive view of what was sometimes called "the national endowment of Romanism," he felt bound to place himself in a position of entire freedom. "Disraeli," writes Lord Morley, "was reported as having said that with his resignation on Maynooth Mr. Gladstone's career was over."

Many years later Mr. Gladstone described his action as one that would be regarded " as fastidious and fanciful, more fit for a dreamer than for the practical purposes of public life." The majority judged it as a display of overstrained moral delicacy, " an act of political prudery." To his adversaries the flavour of the event was ruined by the absence of all bitterness between him and his colleagues.

Characteristically, he would not actually decide on the point at issue till he was detached from a position which might be supposed to bias his mind. When he found himself free from office, he had no difficulty in voting " with emphasis " in support of the Bill. It would be rare nowadays to find a tenderness of conscience so acute as to cause a man to resign office on a measure with which he was really in sympathy. Don Quixote would hardly have been a comfortable colleague in a Cabinet Council.

Macaulay's memorable words are worth recalling at this moment:

" When I remember what was the faith of Edward III. and of Henry VI., of Margaret of Anjou and Margaret of Richmond, of William of Wykeham and Cardinal Wolsey; when I remember what we have taken from the Roman Catholics, King's College, Christ Church, my own Trinity; and when I look at the miserable Dotheboys Hall[1], we have given them in exchange, I feel, I must own, less proud than I could wish of being a Protestant and a Cambridge man."

January 29, 1845.—" William has virtually resigned his seat in the Cabinet on the burning subject of Irish education (the Maynooth Grant), and though he cannot be one of the originators of the Government scheme, it would not be true to say that under existing circumstances he disapproves of their measure. Midst the deep pain he feels it is a comfort to him to reflect that the best understanding exists between him and his friends, and, as ever, he entertains the highest opinion of them; it has been most gratifying to see the warm feelings expressed, and Peel in every way is alive to William's considerate conduct throughout this painful business. He was quite open and unconstrained. J. Shaw-Lefevre, A. Wood, Kinnaird, were here before eleven, and Uncle Tom[2] has just written in greatest anxiety to inquire. Canning has written a beautiful letter, quite to give one a lump in one's throat, indeed I have been living all day with glistening eyes. That kind, hearty Mr. Lefevre—he was turned quite sick. Then William's good little secretary, Mr. Northcote,[3] who could not

---

[1] Maynooth College. [2] Grenville.
[3] Afterwards Sir Stafford, and Earl of Iddesleigh.

Many years' later Mr. Gladstone described his action as one that would be regarded "as fastidious and fanciful, more fit for a dreamer than for the practical purposes of public life." The majority judged it as a display of overstrained moral delicacy, "an act of political prudery." To his adversaries the flavour of the event was ruined by the absence of all bitterness between him and his colleagues.

Characteristically, he would not actually decide on the point at issue till he was detached from a position which might be supposed to bias his mind. When he found himself free from office, he had no difficulty in voting " with emphasis " in support of the Bill. It would be rare nowadays to find a tenderness of conscience so acute as to cause a man to resign office on a measure with which he was really in sympathy. Don Quixote would hardly have been a comfortable colleague in a Cabinet Council.

Macaulay's memorable words are worth recalling at this moment:

" When I remember what was the faith of Edward III. and of Henry VI., of Margaret of Anjou and Margaret of Richmond, of William of Wykeham and Cardinal Wolsey; when I remember what we have taken from the Roman Catholics, King's College, Christ Church, my own Trinity; and when I look at the miserable Dotheboys Hall[1] we have given them in exchange. I feel, I must own, less proud than I could wish of being a Protestant and a Cambridge man."

January 29, 1845.—" William has virtually resigned his seat in the Cabinet on the burning subject of Irish education (the Maynooth Grant), and though he cannot be one of the originators of the Government scheme, it would not be true to say that under existing circumstances he disapproves of their measure. Midst the deep pain he feels it is a comfort to him to reflect that the best understanding exists between him and his friends, and, as ever, he entertains the highest opinion of them; it has been most gratifying to see the warm feelings expressed, and Peel in every way is alive to William's considerate conduct throughout this painful business.' He was quite open and unconstrained. J. Shaw-Lefevre, A. Wood, Kinnaird, were here before eleven, and Uncle Tom[2] has just written in greatest anxiety to inquire. Canning has written a beautiful letter, quite to give one a lump in one's throat, indeed I have been living all day with glistening eyes. That kind, hearty Mr. Lefevre—he was turned quite sick. Then William's good little secretary, Mr. Northcote,[3] who could not

---

[1] Maynooth College.   [2] Grenville.
[3] Afterwards Sir Stafford, and Earl of Iddesleigh.

help breaking down. Lord Dalhousie also much affected."

Mr. Gladstone's own words in a letter to Manning testify to its having been no easy task to part from his own colleagues: "Do you know that daily intercourse and co-operation with men, upon matters of great anxiety and moment, interweaves much of one's being with theirs, and parting with them, leaving them under pressure of work and setting oneself free, feels, I think, much like dying."

In January 1845, Mr. Gladstone went down to Windsor to resign. He wrote to Mrs. Gladstone, describing how the Queen had "brought the little people to the corridor—they behaved very well, shook hands with me by H.M.'s wish. The Prince of Wales has a very good countenance. 'After your own children,' the Queen said, 'you must think them dwarfs.'" She expressed a wish to him that Mrs. Gladstone should bring Willy and Agnes. Accordingly:

"Lady Lyttelton received us, and we took off the children's things before going in to H.M. She shook hands very kindly, and desired me to sit down by her. The three Royal children were with her. Princess Alice a nice fat baby, thoroughly good-humoured and benevolent. Princess Royal about a head shorter than Willy—very engaging, not exactly pretty, but like the Queen and Prince Albert. The Prince of Wales small and the head not striking me as well-shaped, his long trousers, tied below the ankles and very full, most unbecoming. His manners very dear and not shy. They are evidently quite unspoilt, and I observed the Queen made them obey her. Princess Royal and Willy kissed each other, and she patronised little Agnes, who stood by her and the Prince, quite at home and nearly as tall as the Prince, so much so as to make the Queen observe, 'The Prince is the tallest of the two' [he was a year older]. I was much relieved at my children being so good and doing no harm. The Queen observed, 'What care Willy takes of Agnes!' and admired his hair and his width. Agnes's independence amused her, and she was occasionally in fits of laughter at them. Before leaving, the Queen kissed both my children."

Hagley.—" Agnes at four reads easy stories; both have a good ear for music. . . . A month's dissipation at Brighton made Willy too wild, but he is sweet tempered and tractable, though volatile, and has a struggle to fix his attention."

At four Willy begins to ride on a real saddle, and a little later, " sitting capitally, he trotted—only on a horse-cloth."

One more description, three years later, may perhaps be quoted :

January 30, 1846.—" Dined at the Palace. The Queen unbecomingly dressed. Very kind to us, talking much of Mary's children and my own, and for some time to William. The Queen ordered me to bring my children to her on Saturday. I accordingly took the four—Willy, Agnes, Stephy, and Jessy. Her Majesty came in with her four, and was very nice and kind. Princess Royal a nice quick thing; not so much difference in the heights as last time. Prince of Wales has a striking countenance, Alfred very pretty, all have such fat white necks. Prince Alfred is a year and a half old. Stephy head and shoulders taller at one year and ten months. The Queen commented on Agnes's looks, 'I had not heard about her being so very pretty.' Thought Willy pale and Stephen gigantic, baby fat and like her father. She took great notice of them all, kissed Agnes, and gave them a huge white lamb between them all, which the Royal children and ours played with very happily during their visit. The Queen spoke of their goodness, and asked if they were always so good."

March 1847.—" Agnes at four and a half may be led by a silken thread, reads easy lessons with little teaching, and is picking up French quickly; no bump for figures."

In the autumn of 1847, Agnes, five years old, was dangerously ill at Fasque, and when

HAGLEY HALL, STOURBRIDGE
THE HOME OF MARY, LADY LYTTELTON

UNIV. OF
CALIFORNIA

prayed for at a service in the chapel there came a change for the better. Willy, walking with his father: "How lucky it was a saint's day, for you see Agnes is not grand enough to have a service for herself, and if she had not been prayed for she might have died."

1847.—" Arrived at Belvoir Castle, met the Sidney Herberts, Lord Clive, Bishops of Oxford and Lincoln, Lord Forrester, the three sons of the house, and many more of the family. Greatly struck by the grandeur of the situation—dined from twenty to forty each day. Nothing could exceed the Duke's kindness and hospitality. Fascinated by Mrs. Herbert,[1] so pretty and taking—she seems most anxious to do what is right, and was full of the new church at Wilton, the one which is to be consecrated to-morrow."

1848.—" Dined at Sir R. Peel's—an interesting occasion. Anxiety and sorrow sat upon many of the countenances assembled. There stood Guizot, with that piercing eye of fire, his whole appearance eagle-like, his countenance beaming with sagacity and great intellect, in earnest conversation with Peel, full of gesture, and now and then his voice raised, as if bursting with feeling which would out. There were the poor Jarnacs, with full marks

[1] Afterwards Lady Herbert of Lea.

of sorrow for their King and Queen.[1] The Princess Lieven; the Austrian Ambassador, harassed afresh with the increasing troubles in Austria, which so afflicted his wife as to make it impossible for her to be present. The party was relieved by Lord and Lady Aberdeen, Lord and Lady Mahon. I had some talk with Madame Jarnac. Her account of the poor Queen of France especially was touching; of the dangers and trials connected with their flight, of the sad deprivations to which they were subject, the terror of the poor Queen about her husband [2] and then her children. . . . Sir Robert Peel joined in our conversation. He views the state of Europe with much alarm. He had received private information respecting the Prince of Prussia (now at Bunsen's) who is said to have broken his sword and laid it, with his spurs, at the feet of the King of Prussia.

"Lady Peel looks wonderfully young and pretty."

Dining with the Prime Minister, the conversation turned on " subjects which especially brought out feeling—his children and their education. He enlarged on the satisfaction of having no permanent governess, liked his girls to travel with him, said it enlarged their minds, and much more—showing that amidst

---

[1] Revolution of 1848.   [2] Louis Philippe.

his great cares the domestic element is deep in his heart."

January 1849.—" Stephy at five and a half is a curious child. I feel there is much to come out of him and he will not be commonplace. Feelings warm, kindness and what he may think unkindness sink very deep. There is much in him for good or for evil."

Fasque. 1849.—" Willy writes to Charles, bursting with happiness—tells how he has a hundred amusements and occupations. . . . He goes daily now to his father for his Latin lesson. His father tells me his choice of language is remarkable; but he is not one who makes the most of himself. I sometimes fear he will do himself injustice. He reads the Bible to blind Peter on Sunday evenings— dear boy, he goes to school ($9\frac{1}{2}$) next month. May God keep him safe."

His parents were much pleased a few years later when, at the age of seventeen, Willy was chosen by the Queen to accompany the Prince of Wales on his first tour abroad. The friendship was continued at Christ Church and after.

In the summer of 1849, Mr. Gladstone, at the instigation of his wife, left England and travelled across Europe in hopes of discovering and saving a lady who had left her husband. The husband was one of his most trusted friends and colleagues, while the wife was very dear to Mrs. Gladstone. This quixotic mission was undertaken at the earnest wish of the husband, and both Mr. and Mrs. Gladstone would leave no stone unturned in bringing about a reconciliation between the two. The story is told by Lord Morley in vol. i. of his biography of Mr. Gladstone.[1] It was part of the work of rescue that ever lay so close to their hearts : it was characteristic of both that, rich or poor, humble or exalted, the appeal was never made in vain.

Mrs. Gladstone's notes on their fourth child, Jessy, show her, in her first two years, to have been quicker and more eager and passionately loving than the elder ones. But gradually a cloud seemed to settle upon this interesting child and she grew quiet and drowsy, her eyes grave and wistful—"Dormouse," as some one called her at that time. "At four years old she is very picturesque, with her curly hair and so pretty in her Rubens hat, peculiarly loving, watching me like a cat and taking tender care of me. Blessed child, I can see her now, watching my every movement for the chance of going with me. At Hagley, when she was so unwell and it hurt her to walk, she would follow me, sweet lamb, to my room and sit happy in the arm-chair, living as it were on a word or look of mine. I can hear

[1] P. 364.

her saying, 'Dear sweet Mammy, you look so kind at me.' She was a darling baby. With what double pleasure, during her father's absence, did I gaze at her, tracing his image in her face—often it came across me that there would be a solidity of character about my Jessy, there was such earnestness in the large, serious eyes."

For the first ten years all had gone radiantly with both families, and nothing but ephemeral anxieties came their way. It was early in 1850 that death first cast its shadow over the Gladstone household and their beloved child, Catherine Jessy, developed meningitis at the age of four and a half years. It has been related that for some hours after her death (April 1850) her father was in a state of such violent grief as almost to frighten those around him.

But suddenly his sense of duty got the upper hand. Thenceforward he was calm, and under the stress of deep emotion he put on paper a record of the little life; it might rank with the immortal description written by De Quincey when death first touched his household.

But Mrs. Gladstone's own pathetic words can be quoted here: "I dread lest the solemn remembrance of her loved face after death should in any way fade, so holy, so heavenly it was. My loved child—my own Jessy, to think that the quiet countenance in such deep repose is the same which a few hours ago was racked with pain. The hair lay curling on the marble forehead, the long dark lashes fringing her cheek, the little hands folded across one another, roses and lilies of the valley about her. I could not describe the sublimity of her expression."

And then she copies out the closing words of her husband's little memoir:

"The countenance was holy, it was heavenly—it blessed the eyes that saw it. It was a voiceless yet speaking expression, and its meaning was this—'I have seen the things that ye know not of: I have tasted of the Eternal Peace. I have seen my Lord and my God, and I am with Him for ever.'

"It bore witness to the promise, 'He shall gather the lambs within His arm. He shall carry them in His bosom.'

"It answered the prayer which during her restlessness and pain so often rose instinctively to our lips:

"' Jesu bone, bone Jesu, Pastor ovium, Pastor agnorum, miserere.'"[1]

---

[1] Jesu holy, holy Jesu, Shepherd of the sheep, Shepherd of the lambs, have mercy upon us.

CHAPTER IV

LETTERS FROM HER

MRS. GLADSTONE had a well-earned reputation for making bricks without straw. Certainly her letters, written anywhere, any time, anyhow, with totally inadequate materials, were miracles of expression. She wrote with facility and felicity, and was possessed of a rapid and expressive pen. To each of her daughters she wrote several thousand letters, her sons have as great a number, and many of her nieces and friends could say the same. In three words she gave a living picture—not so much facts, perhaps, as atmosphere. Nothing escaped her quick eye. She touched off with a masterly hand scenes, people, talks. To-day she would be classed as a first-rate Impressionist. Whenever absent from her, so long as one had the newspapers for facts and her letters for comments and atmosphere, one really seemed to know more, to be more *au fait*, than even when with her. And in spite of an elliptical and allusive style, apart from the Glynnese slang, her English and her grammar were pure.

A year or two ago her daughter made an attempt to go through her own letters from her mother. In the midst of this task she dashed off an account of it to Lady Frederick Cavendish.

Of her own and her sister's children—hers all but in name—one only inherits much of Catherine Gladstone's nature, her largeness of heart, her divine compassion, her sanguine temperament, her raciness of speech, her impetuosity, her disregard of appearances— and this was Lucy, Lady Frederick Cavendish. It may throw some light on the subject to give this letter *in extenso*:

"I am looking over her letters, a really appalling job, as there are *thousands*, and you, better than anyone, know the rags and tatters they are written on, the atrocious pens, the smudges and blots, no stops, the 'i's' never dotted, the 't's' never crossed: one requires a daily journal of the House of Commons' doings and another of families—yours, ours, Stepneys, Talbots, Gladstones, Dumaresques, Farquhars, Cavendishes, etc., all to whom she was mother, friend, angel. And yet another volume of benevolent doings.

"The frequent lack of nominative cases, the

allusions, the hints, the flying remarks, and sketches and pen-pictures, and comparisons and suggestions and descriptions, enigmatic, elliptic, elusive, her finger literally on the pulse of the House of Commons—far more brilliant even than I had remembered, but buried in yards and yards of plans, accounts, domestic details, like brilliant fragments dug up in ancient Greece or Rome. They literally palpitate with life, they catch the very breath of the moment, they are essentially written for that moment only; they require the people, the tendencies, the thoughts, the feelings, the enthusiasms, the emotions, the thrills of that moment; the spiciness depends on the homeliness or intimacy of the touch, the humour of the happenings, the expressions —Glynnese, Boffin,[1] or medical. The aroma vanishes if brought into the public eye.

"One of the most amazing things is how he bore it, the endless chars[2] and jobs-she put on him for charity or kindness, the manœuvres behind his back, the extraordinary dodges to smooth his path or oil his wheels or cocker up his health, the astonishing intricacy of her arrangements, the dovetailing and never-ceasing attempts to fit in things which couldn't and wouldn't fit ! The never losing a chance or

[1] See *Our Mutual Friend*: "In the presence of Mrs. Boffin we had better drop the subject."
[2] "Odd jobs done for others but not for him."—*Glynnese Glossary.*

an opportunity of helping somebody, however remote or far-fetched; the tucking in or tucking up of incongruous people, so long as they were troubled or in difficulties of sorts. . . .

"'Could you order some tooth-brushes and brushes *cheap* for the Orphanage?' she wrote to him. 'Have you remembered to peep in on the Miss D.'s?[1] Only open the boudoir door and you will find them.' 'Did you manage the flowers (or grapes) for Mrs. Bagshawe? She lives quite near Portland Place.' 'If you have *time*, please bring down a little present for my three-year-old godchild [a curate's baby]; there are beautiful Bible prints at the Sanctuary, Westminster, and also we want a common easel from the same place, 5s. to 8/6, to hold the big maps for the boys.'

"Why didn't it drive him wild, with the direct and 'radiant simplicity' of his character? No amount of experience made him suspicious. Two things saved the situation and rendered him impervious to her pranks—his sense of humour and his heart of gold. Still it is bewildering—she lived a hundred lives at one go.

"But what strikes me afresh and anew is how marvellously, miraculously you jumped

---

[1] Two very poor Italian ladies secreted in Downing Street, ostensibly as caretakers.

with her, crept with her, flew with her. Whatever her pace, you kept up; whatever she needed, there you were, living, so to speak, in her pocket, always ready to fall in with her and dovetail, and swap butlers, and supply meals, beds, cooks, or carriages at a moment's notice. Was ever a miraculous aunt so blessed with a miraculous niece?—and Freddy,[1] who might have been driven crazy, loved it, revelled in it, enjoyed it to the hilt. Can't you see his wink and hers? Can't you hear his laughter as he writhed with amusement over her description of a scene at Falconhurst, when she would call the tame little wood the jungle? Even this hurried little scrawl (enclosed) bubbles over with characteristic touches—the sudden arrival at your house, the scrambled hiding of the bulk of his letters, the blank for the secretary's name, the little bleat after her absent lamb, the thrilling scene at Euston (no one out of office nowadays could arouse that frantic enthusiasm)."

The following letter was written by one of her sons,[2] who had attempted to tackle his own "library of letters" from her:

"All so very personal, some so sacred, and much only likely to interest nears and

---

[1] Lord Frederick Cavendish.   [2] Rev. Stephen Gladstone.

dears. The industry in writing is as extraordinary as the depth of love. It has truly been a sacred privilege, not short of a revelation, to read this library of letters again, throwing such intense light of truth and love shed by this mother of mothers on my poor life. Quite a new revelation in addition to past influences. But the personal character, the watchful care and deep devotion, as expressed in words, are only meant for us.

"But many things astonish me—little and great. Endless instances of how thoughtful, clear, and exact she was about making plans, often under very intricate and varying circumstances. So *rangé* in her thoughtfulness, so business-like in her schemes, so penetrating her sympathy and insight; so keen for moral growth in her love. . . . All silent now and far removed. Yet that great heart beats more than ever now."

But there is one short set of letters, written to her husband on the proposed resignation of the leadership, which strikes a more consecutive note.

In January 1875, she was at Hawarden just after her husband had told her that the time of his formal resignation of the leadership of the Liberal party was at hand. It was nine months after the General Election of

1874, when the trump card of his Address was the offer, for the first time in it's history, to do away altogether with the Income Tax. His Government had accomplished mighty things. In Ireland the anomaly of a Protestant Church dominating an overwhelmingly Roman Catholic country had been removed.[1] Free National Education had been given to Great Britain.[2] Purchase in the Army had been abolished (1873). Arbitration as a governing principle in disputed international questions had been established.[3] 'Independence and secrecy in voting had been ensured.[4] Mr. Gladstone had paid twenty-six millions off the National Debt. He left a surplus of five millions to his successors. He looked forward, if returned to power, to abolishing the Income Tax. Such performance and promise, surely, as has been seldom marshalled before a country. But the country was sick and tired of economy and reform. The General Election gave a majority of fifty to his opponents.

The deep desire of his heart for respite from controversy, as a preparation for death, was, without any doubt, the leading motive of his resignation at the comparatively early age of sixty-five.

[1] Disestablishment and disendowment of the Irish Church.
[2] Mr. Forster's Education Act, 1870.
[3] Alabama Claims, 1873.   [4] The Ballot Act.

Mrs. Gladstone had left London at the crisis and had gone to Hagley to nurse a dearly loved niece. The following letters, or portions of letters, were written to him by her in January 1875:—

On Mr. Gladstone's Resignation of the Leadership

"*January* 7.

"I know full well your whole soul is bent upon doing right. You would go to the death in a righteous cause. Who could hold you when the battle-cry sounded? I expressed myself so badly in the hurry of parting—alas, it seemed to you I was going against you, and that my judgment was formed! Perhaps from the very fact of my longing to see you rest and to acquiesce in all your wishes, I felt it the greater duty to look well on all sides; and remember, there are those who can speak more frankly to me than to you, and who desire your honourable course of action. Is there not something to be said against your own point, which strengthens their argument in this shape? Great Church questions may arise when your power and influence would be valuable. Would you have the same power by a sudden rush to fight after *putting the reins upon others*? The party would naturally be at sea. Is there no medium course? What necessity would there be for constant attendance? Who would expect it? Could you not take it quite easily? Would not the patience and calmness and modesty of your attitude speak, not only to the House of Commons, but to the whole country? No doubt there is a feeling that you only care about *fights* now—*that* would take away this idea: to see you so patient, so good, sacrificing your own wishes and only helping others, accepting the position and meeting it. May it not be right? Is not the position, so to speak, forced upon you? If you had any organic illness which made it wrong for you to expose your precious life, it would be different. Dr. Clark[1] spoke to me last year quite in an opposite sense. These little ailments are just safety valves. Some have giddiness in the head, or palpitations of the heart, and no warning but the danger; in your ailment, you have time to pull up and get right. You say if you take the lead you are there for ever. Why, who would say a word against your giving up, if health really demanded it? I was saying to Edward Talbot how you yearned for rest from strife, and I suggested Hartington as leader. He said: " I, at all events, am a fair and impartial person as to politics, and knowing how Mr. G. might

[1] Sir Andrew Clark, M.D.

have to do things for conciliation that I might disapprove, I still feel his importance to the country as leader so strongly that I hope he will not shrink." He thought many people would explain your resigning as a religious mania, and that this would undermine your influence, whilst by proving you can calmly attend to political business in Opposition you would double your influence when needed.

"I hope I have not troubled you with my twaddle. At all events you may feel that I write with the one object that you may be guided aright to the glory of God and the good of your fellow creatures. That your acquiescing would be unselfish to the highest degree—I know that well. At all events, you will forgive me. Do not write about it till you have seen Lord Granville again: it only takes out of you, which is the last thing I wish."

"*January* 12, 1875.

"First, it is a great deal too much to say that you and I take different views of this important question of the leadership. It could not be so, as I had by no means made up my own mind. But I did consider it my duty to lay before you the drawbacks; and that you should receive from me the unbiassed opinion of what might be thought, and so weigh the matter. Perhaps I am too sensitive in the feeling of anything like running away, when the road is dark and hopeless. I believe (though perhaps I should fail) that I have looked upon your career very much as that of a general in a dangerous battle, whether winning or losing. However, my poor opinion is so little worth having, perhaps I need not have said anything; but I like you to know that we do not really differ, more than from the great desire, the trembling desire, you should do right; and thus I wished to act as a kind of drag on so important a step. God will bless and help you as He has done in mighty decisions, and be what it may, I am content.

"In the meantime I delight in your report of Clark's opinion. Killing, your saying he does not take so rosy a view of the trouble as I do. All I mean is that there could not be a safer vent, and, as you seldom rest your dear head, I am patient over this vent, and thank God for Clark's word '*Excellent.*' Am I not borne out that it would be a quiz [1] for you to have pleaded health as a reason? And the thing I really desire everywhere is less high pressure, more calmness in work, and more allowance of relaxation."

[1] *Glynnese Glossary.*

"*January* 16, 1875.

"What a jolly letter! Quite human. So dear of you to give me such a treat! Yesterday's letter will show you I am 'perfectly content.' You did not see that it was rather as the martyr I took up the argument. It was not, I think, ambition, except in the best sense of the word. . . . The Spencers want us to go to Althorp on the 25th. That would be flesh[1]; if on our way to London it might be different."

It was not the first time or the last that a man, not yet old, who had been Prime Minister, resigned the leadership for the shades of Opposition, to return to it a few years later at a great crisis. Mr. Gladstone resigned in January 1875, and two years had barely elapsed before the great crisis (Eastern Question) called him back. In five years he was again Prime Minister. Mr. Balfour resigned in 1911, at the age of sixty-four, also while in Opposition. A great crisis called him back, and he took office under Mr. Asquith in 1915.

Some specimens may be selected from her more normal letters—letters written under

---

[1] "An exceedingly rare idiom, the use of which is perhaps confined to Mrs. Gladstone. It refers to money payments and means actual hard money out of pocket, and is said to be an allusion, more poetic than precise, to the story of Shylock."—*Glynnese Glossary.*

CATHERINE GLADSTONE
1856
From a portrait by Say at Hawarden

more favourable circumstances, such as a well-appointed writing-table, a good quill—she never used a steel pen—some unwonted leisure, and circumstances that appealed to her heart. The Royal visits, of which there are several accounts, fulfilled these conditions perhaps best of all, and such letters are of more public interest than some of those written from other houses.

It has already been said that Mrs. Gladstone and Lady Lyttelton when apart never allowed one day to pass without writing to each other. But these letters are specially unquotable, so intimate, often so sacred, so ephemeral they are.

Taken at random from a heap of old letters at Hagley, one specimen may be quoted on account of its historical value.

CATHERINE TO MARY
"*March* 1854.

"MY LOVE,—Our anxiety is at an end for the present, but oh, how it wears one out ! . . . They say it is all her doing. Lord John is firm one moment, then he goes home and she sits upon him—the whole thing being then set to wrongs again. However, as you will see, he did end by giving in, and the Reform Bill is dropped. We were with Lady John in the House. Poor Lord John did well, but he broke down at last and wept so as not to be able to rally. They cheered and cheered, but still his voice was *entrecoupé*, and he never recovered. Upstairs, in the Speaker's Gallery, Lady John wept too, and I leave it to your imagination to fancy the scene. Well, I had to go alone[1] to the Queen, very small and very pleasant, but I have no time to write the account I should wish. As there were no big-wigs I had nice conversation with the Queen.[2] The points most interesting for you are these: 'How well your sister looks; and Albert, he is quite handsome. I had no idea he could turn out anything like that. . . . Meriel is too like her grandmama,[3] but Lucy is pretty (or very pretty—I forget exactly). Where does Lord Lyttelton get his peculiar manner from?' I answered, 'Oh, ma'am, everything about him is good; it is delightful to see him with his children.' The Queen bowed her head in assent. I cannot tell you how I admire her extreme simplicity—my great difficulty is to keep in remembrance that she is Queen. In the middle of talking, H.M. said, 'Oh, I must just run and have my gown fastened.' Very nice, too, she

[1] Mr. Gladstone was ill.
[2] Among Queen Victoria's letters to Mrs. Gladstone there are several that refer to their long friendship. In 1885, H.M. reminded her that fifty years had elapsed since she first met "the beautiful Miss Glynnes" at Bishopthorpe, in 1835.
[3] Dowager Lady Lyttelton.

MARY, LADY LYTTELTON
1857
From a portrait by Say at Hagley

was about William; in short, I really enjoyed. it, in spite of having felt so *dépourvu*.

"The Duchess of Sutherland [1] insisted on returning home with me to see how William was. Fancy me entering his room with her, I fully expecting to find him in his old dressing-gown, with one candle—in short, *unearthly* ! [2] We seated her upon the stool of repentance, her petticoats tipping over everything. William and Willy [3] meanwhile devouring their mutton chops."

Catherine and Mary had lived so much with their mother at her beautiful home at Audley End that the Neville sons were to them more like brothers than cousins. The following letter, written in 1855, from Catherine to Mary, speaks of their acute anxiety about Grey and Henry, two of the sons serving in the Crimean War:

"I have been dining with Mrs. Charles Neville, in search of information how to send Grey books and comforts. They won't believe that Henry is not killed, and their agony of suspense is awful. Poor Uncle Braybrooke keeps on saying, 'If I could only know what

---

[1] Duchess Harriet, Mistress of the Robes, the devoted friend of Mr. Gladstone and of Garibaldi.
[2] *Glynnese Glossary.*
[3] William Henry, their eldest son, aged thirteen.

has happened, I feel I could bear it better.' And she has chlorosene, which only makes it worse. We cannot hear more before Wednesday, and if it is at all good news, we mean to telegraph to Audley End. When Henry wrote on the fourth he was well, and most thankful to have no more trench work, the Turks having been put to that. He described it as awful, waiting in cold blood to have your head blown off, far worse than a field of battle —at times not daring to keep one's head up lest a shell should blow it off. All this acts on the nerves, as you may suppose. Grey is so tall, so slim, his constitution may not stand it. Henry much stronger. Grey[1] is twenty-three, and Mirabel[2] always looks upon him almost as a child. She is calm, but we see how she suffers. I hope I shall get leave for this little parcel of books to go out to him, besides the other parcel of a warm dressing-gown, poor dear fellow. Again we have a Cabinet to-day. Here is an interesting letter from Miss Nightingale, dated Constantinople, on board the *Victory*, which I send you as a curiosity."

The following letter, written on August 6, 1861, from Hawarden, refers to the death, four

[1] Grey and Henry were both killed.
[2] Their sister, whose hair turned white from this agony. Both her brothers were killed, at Inkermann and Balaclava.

days earlier, of Sidney Herbert, companion and colleague, the godfather of one of their sons, their next-door neighbour in Carlton Gardens, and perhaps their most intimate and best-beloved, friend :

"To-day brings me touching accounts from Wilton — so resembling Hagley, it is moving to the last degree — and the same month too.[1] His begging their pardon for keeping them watching so long—'I am sorry it is so protracted'—and entreating them not to tire themselves—' I never thought that dying would be so difficult an operation, my poor darlings—it is so hard upon you all; but I am happy, quite happy.' I keep the letters for you. I much wish you could sleep at Wilton; you might be a help to her, and they would never have asked you had they not wished it."

Here are her comments on his visit to Windsor, one year only after they were last there together in the Prince Consort's lifetime.

"*October* 1862.

". . . I like to feel you can be a comfort to that darling Queen, and I know you can. You will take in that this is nearly the anniversary of our visit, when all was still bright. I was looking back to the little notes I made

[1] Mary Lyttelton died in August 1857 (see page 279, Chap. VIII.).

the last time that we were to meet on earth. The Prince Consort happened to be speaking to me about fevers and Lord Aberdeen and Peel, and I tried to remember his conversation with you about the American War. You said to me afterwards you liked to think of it as one of his last. . . . Now, contrary to your ways, do pet the Queen, and for once believe you can, you dear old thing."

A month later she writes of the "little boys,"[1] nine and ten years old, first going to school: "We have tried on the new jackets and trousers, and a bathing feel[2] and a gulp could not be helped! Dear little fellows, God bless and prosper them! I did long for you to see them. On Sunday they beg to go to church in their school clothes, and I mean to be very brave; indeed, they will look very touching, but it is trying the going away of the youngest pair, and the first launching of them into the world. You do understand, and will not think me very weak if I own to crying at the very thought—that other boy, too, just at the same moment hundreds of miles off riding upon the waves—a continual storm in my ears."

There is a pathetic account of her first

[1] Harry and Herbert. [2] See *Glynnese Glossary*.

interview with Queen Victoria after the death of the Prince Consort. She quotes her husband's words after seeing Her Majesty on March 22, 1862—three months after she became a widow.

"I was really bewildered," he wrote, "but all that vanished when the Queen came in and held my hand a moment. All was beautiful, simple, noble, and touching to the very last degree. I need only repeat the first and last words. The first (putting down her head and struggling), 'The nation has been very good to me in my sorrow'; the last, 'I earnestly pray it may be long before you are parted from one another.'"

After the interview this message reached Mr. Gladstone: "Of all her Ministers, she seemed to feel that you had entered most into her sorrows : she dwelt especially on the manner in which you had parted with her." He left her astonished at her humility. "It was impossible not to be deeply stirred by her noble sorrow."

"The first sight of her was so piteous," wrote Mrs. Gladstone. "She saw I was nervous, and when I kissed her hand drew me to her and kissed me. 'After all, I am but a wretched woman,' she said. 'You who are such a loving wife, I knew how you would feel for me,' and she gazed at me with tears in her eyes; there seemed so heavenly an expression, a look beyond this world, and all the time such gentle kindness and submission. She spoke of the sympathy she had always felt for widows. At the first moment of his peril she had uttered, 'You cannot tell me that I am to lose him.' Princess Alice was the one to break the reality to her mother. She told me that she could only bear it from feeling it was but for a time. She dwelt upon the awful loneliness, how that the daily life together had grown into a very part of her being—now she had no one to tell things to. 'Anything new, any change is a great trial,' she said. She spoke of the help it was to go on with his wishes, to carry out and finish his plans. 'Yes, this helps me on, and there is another thing helps. It is extraordinary how I cannot help constantly expecting to find him—whether it is out walking, near some tree or some flower, or sitting in some particular spot, or coming into the room and hearing his footstep.'

"As the Queen spoke she would grow quite animated, with the idea almost as if she was going to see him. Then the countenance changed again to sadness. She asked me much about my sister, whether she had suffered. I told her how once my darling had said, 'I had no idea there could be such suffering.' The Queen looked full of pity. I often feel if the Prince had tried to live, if he had had more nervous energy, he might perhaps have recovered. She had already spoken of his having had no fear of death, and reasoned upon it as the more remarkable that ' he was far from being one that had no pleasure or interest in life.' "

Later, the Queen wrote Mr. Gladstone a letter of " passionate desolation." She ends: " Mrs. Gladstone, who is a most tender wife, may in a faint measure picture what the Queen suffers."

In October 1861 the distress in Lancashire reached a climax. The American Civil War had arrested the supply of cotton, and pretty nearly produced something like famine in Lancashire. Mr. and Mrs. Gladstone set a scheme on foot for the employment of Lancashire operatives, and they had enlisted the co-operation of Lord Westminster, Sir John Hamner, and others of their neighbours, and collected a considerable sum of money. The men were to be employed on the several estates, and at Hawarden Mrs. Gladstone and her brothers marked out new walks winding through some of the most entrancing spots in the park. Mrs. Gladstone went off to investigate for herself the condition of the cotton towns of Lancashire, and from her letters her husband formed the highest opinion of the " passive fortitude " of the sufferers under conditions of acute distress. " Self-command, respect for order, patience under suffering, confidence in the law." In the middle of November she writes to him from Blackburn, and mentions how she is keeping the Queen informed of the condition of the population. She speaks of the great joy and comfort given by the Queen's sympathy and her messages to the sufferers. She visited the poor people in their homes, and describes the wonderful way " the men plod to church to listen to their rector's words of exhortation and hope. It was very edifying to see their attentiveness, but moving to the last degree to notice the pale, emaciated faces and the look of sadness—yet a resigned look, too. Dr. Robinson asked me to speak to them, and there was nothing for it but to try—simple and short; indeed, I felt ready to cry as I noticed one man in tears. God will help them. 'Yes, these are times no one can ever forget; they will do us good,' said another man. One of them spoke of the text, 'Strive ye to enter in.' 'We must not think of the great cost if it is to lead us to heaven. Oh, one ought to be the better for all this experience.'"

November 17.—" A very overpowering day; in truth, I am tired and cannot do justice to the scenes. I had to make another very little speech to-day to the poor men. Their grateful looks are so touching; but the extent of the misery goes to one's very heart—the sadness, the endurance. The Mayor came and thanked them all for me. Three hearty cheers and then one more for you for sending me here."

From Blackburn she proceeded to Preston, Darwin, and Ashton-under-Lyne. " A most interesting day, seeing, investigating, advising." She gives touching instances of her experiences :

" When I told her I would take the child, the emotion was too much, she fell upon her knees —and there are hundreds of such cases of silent, uncomplaining misery." During her progress she caught a chill, completely losing her voice, but still persevered.

" I just managed Staley Bridge on the 20th, and realised Dr. Whittaker's noble doings. I was actually sick between acts, managing to hide in a quiet room and then to emerge later and appear better, *comme si rien n'était!*

When I reached Stockport I was, alas! compelled to give in and make my excuses. I should not presume to think my going or not going could be of consequence, only the kind feelings for my name, really for your sake, seem to have swelled into something (for me) very big."

Mrs. Gladstone got up a concert at Hawarden for the benefit of the Lancashire distress, when she arranged that the poor factory girls should go on to the platform in their working clothes, their shawls over their heads. They sang "Hard Times" with pathetic fervour, and the whole audience was moved to tears.

In her frequent visits to Windsor and Osborne she makes many shrewd remarks about the Queen, always struck by her simplicity and sincerity, her common sense. "I never hear her talk without feeling one ought to be the better for it, she is *so true.*" She quotes a remark of Her Majesty's during the American War, advising carefulness in judgment. "I am afraid," she said, "we are very apt to have one law for ourselves and another for other people." "The way H.M. discusses things always interests me, arguing her own points and listening to the differences of others, all the time with a certain decision of manner." She comments on the charm and happiness of the Prince and Princess of Prussia. The Princess took her to her own suite of rooms at Windsor to see her works of art. "I have never been able to afford to have the casts made into marble," she said. "We have so many expenses—children—journeys, etc."

The winning simplicity of the family circle strikes her. The Queen's relations with her sons-in-law recalls the Duchess of Sutherland's footing with the Duke of Argyll. The delight of the advent of the Danish bride, her beauty, her brightness, her fun. In 1871, when Mrs. Gladstone was at Osborne, the Queen was most anxious the public should realise how devotedly the Princess of Wales nursed her husband the same year in his dangerous illness, how she never left him day or night. That apparently people imagined it was his sister, Princess Alice of Hesse, who nursed him. She begged Mrs. Gladstone to take every opportunity of making this known.

"HAWARDEN, *June* 9, 1879.

"——'s letters [from Faringford] are capital —the second surpassing the first. Tennyson loves them both, and is more quaint than ever— examines ——'s features, treats her as a child, is amused at what he calls her *petit nez retroussé;* says its wickedness is counteracted by her strong jawbone."

In 1883 she meets at Osborne the three Princesses, daughters of Princess Alice of Hesse, her husband sitting between them at dinner, and describes specially the second—" a very striking face, fine speaking eyes, a dear manner, listens with that eager attention that brings out the expression of her countenance. The third daughter quite as natural and nice, good countenance, simple, and forthcoming." How little could then be guessed the tragic fate that awaited them in Russia !

To force the Sultan (specially in his promises regarding Greece and Montenegro) to carry out the provisions of the Treaty of Berlin [1] Mr. Gladstone's Government in October 1880, more or less backed by the Concert of Europe, threatened to blockade Smyrna. Each Power had sent a man-of-war to the Albanian coast. Turkey, thoroughly alarmed, to the boundless satisfaction of the Prime Minister, gave way, the Greek frontier was rectified, practically realising Mr. Gladstone's dream of a Homeric Greece, and Dulcigno was ceded to Montenegro.

"HAWARDEN, *October* 11, 1880.

" After being in bed with this tiresome throat, ' joy did come in the morning.' Oh,

[1] 1879.

your large sheet and its contents and Hymn of Praise! For His power has wrought wonders.

> 'We praise Thee and will praise Thee,
> We bless Thee and will bless,
> We give thanks to Thee and will give thanks.'

"And you, dearest own, who have mercifully been permitted to take part in such mighty operations! What shall I say? It is almost too much to think of this consummation. The 'ideal of your life' in foreign policy, God only grant it may be all right and no more bolting. But if he[1] does bolt on learning more as to the cowardly Powers, my hope even then is that the Powers may have had the warning from the Sultan's white feather, and join issue at once. You see I am arming myself for contingencies. We shall be all ready for you to-morrow.

"The Flowers[2] came to hand yesterday in time for a lovely glow of sunshine which lighted up garden and Castle and all. They are very light in hand and easily pleased, but disappointed that you are away. I have been silent and dull until you open my lips as to Smyrna and Ireland, for though the paper has it, of course, that is different from my confirmation! Doubly careful with Lady Herbert.... The Flowers are very large-

---

[1] The Sultan.   [2] Afterwards Lord and Lady Battersea.

hearted people, full of good deeds, coffee-houses, hospitals, etc."

To M. G.

"SANDRINGHAM; *November* 21, 1880.

" Here we are, somehow we hated the start, early at station, cold east wind, so we got chilled, travelled with the Granvilles—I feel I appreciate her much more. King's Lynn gave us a reception—nice to see the people hunting for him patiently in the cold, in the way you know so well. Ely Cathedral, though nearly in the dark, stood grandly and looked majestic. As we entered the hall (with my usual arriving feelings) we were met by the darling hostess, the Prince of Wales, Duke of Edinburgh, and last, not least, dear little trio of Princesses, the eldest twelve—all so homey. Princess so dear, and different to London, came to our rooms upstairs and said to Stüme,[1] who curtseyed in the corner; she hoped that 'all was comfy' (fancy her delight). Lovely flowers in my bedroom. I sat by Prince of Wales and Dr. Acland at dinner — afterwards we chatted abundantly, Princess showing me her sitting-room and her collections—she is the most dear homey thing, full of her sons, who have left home for eighteen months. The eldest,

[1] A faithful maid with her for twenty years.

MRS. GLADSTONE AND HER SON HERBERT
1861

CALIFOR
UNIV.

Prince Eddy, doats on his mother. He said in his last letter: 'Darling mother dear,—I smelt some scent which you always use, and it made me so sad.'

"Father is to read the Lessons by order of Prince and Princess. A bright, glorious cold day, and we are just going to church. . . . We are back—you will have the first lesson fresh in your heart and mind—'In the sight of the unwise.' 'Stir up' Sunday. Think of the words coming from father's lips, the pathos and glorious emphasis. The Princess chooses the hymns always, and to-day had taken the greatest pains to select his (father's) favourites — 'Rock of Ages' and 'Lead, Kindly Light.' Wasn't it pretty? The Memorial to her baby just behind the Princess, 'Suffer Little Children' and Our Lord receiving the baby. Singing very pretty and all reverently, nicely done — the Altar with Cross and flowers. Father very happy. They made me play at bowls!

"Mind you arrange I should see you on my way to Wellington and give you the birthday kiss."

In November 1880 she mentions a dinner at the Childers'.[1] "Very interesting, I sitting next to Sir F. Roberts. I liked him *extremely*,

[1] Minister for War.

so modest, pacific seemingly as to Ireland, which won my heart. Who should walk in after dinner (only ladies present) but Sir Bartle Frere [1]—his daughter beamed, and I had to say something nice to him, at the risk of his not knowing me. Duke of Cambridge whispering and touching one's face. Mrs. Childers triumphant, Dufferins, Morleys. I liked young Childers, the lad who was at Eton with Harry and Herbert. He is just back from India with Sir F. R.—and evidently a sort of right hand to him. . . . . Father just out of Cabinet, Ministers looking relieved. . . . . To-morrow we go to Convalescent Home to see the new room."

To M. D.

"SANDRINGHAM, *January* 29, 1887.

"Here we are in spite of yesterday's scrimmage, for upon waking father was not well. I sent for Clark (perturbation), *he* meanwhile hoping to get off coming here — all ended well, and our journey was easy and luxurious — grand saloon carriage and the Prince in another. Good Bishop Claughton with us—he thrills over Lucy; give her his best love. Great demonstrations at Cam-

---

[1] Recalled from the Governorship of South Africa by Mr. Gladstone's Government.

bridge (where we shot out Helen into the arms of admiring crowds), at Ely, and King's Lynn. Eddie Hamilton tells me the Prince of Wales was very good-natured as to the great crowds and cheering for father, and was much interested to see it. It felt very queer with a· Prince of Wales in the offing. All kindness he was; took me and Madame de Falbe in his carriage from the station to the House; so genial and kind. Fancy her turning out to have been Mrs. Dudley Ward, who sang years ago at our house. I sat at dinner between Prince of Wales and Prince Eddy. I had some interesting talk with the former about Randolph; he seems to take his part. . . . Just come from church in carriage with darling Princess — more dear than ever. She was quite full of your illness. Old ——— in white damask last night, hair carefully arranged and fuzzed, looking quite young behind. We all sang. I pretending to, to please Princess. Princess of Wales accompanying three daughters, Falbe and I in a sort of mad glee till the men came in. . . ."

"SANDRINGEAM, *January* 30.

" We have had a very nice visit here. There is really nothing like this Royal home—such simplicity and reality and thought for others.

I am struck by their having people who fitted. Eddie H. and dear Bishop Claughton. He is all tenderness, and so interested in our going back to Hawarden for the Mission. No trace of ailment. Tell Lucy his luncheon before starting was arrowroot and brandy; he is to have as little butter as possible, and less tea. But I am more than thankful seeing how entirely he was in his own force and form in House of Commons—voice excellent, something peculiarly dignified in his speech. Fancy Lady Pembroke and Adelaide [1] admiring, though of course not agreeing. In the meantime, Helen and I were trembling as to Cambridge. Dr. Clark rather shaken as to whether he could do it all after Sandringham."

(*Finished at Newnham College*)

"I am to dine with the students, father in Hall with Dr. Butler, then to come here to tea and bed. So pretty to see the girls playing in the garden. Father happy in his pretty, tiny dressing-room. No one could explain all this [2]—one must see it to understand. Certainly Helen wins their hearts, and they win hers. There is no doubt of this, and there is such ease about it all, every one is natural."

[1] Lady Brownlow.   [2] Women's Colleges.

"NEWNHAM COLLEGE, CAMBRIDGE,
"*January* 31, 1887.

"We are to meet some thrilling company again at tea, father and all. Yesterday we went to King's. Oh! the *Nunc dimittis*, too lovely. How glorious the organ and the whole building, lifting one up! It is extraordinary the feeling for father. He is so well, and enters, as you know, into everything. Kathleen awfully kind, and you and Lucy will delight in hearing how much struck we are with dear Arthur's[1] whole bearing—the right man in the right place. Father says he fills it just as you would most desire.

"What fine children the Lytteltons — nice and affectionate and unshy."

In another letter from Sandringham she describes a knock at the door just as she was ready for bed. In walked the Princess, and H.R.H. was not satisfied till she had tucked her up in bed.

"HAWARDEN, 1887.

"Oh, can you believe it? We hear that the Duke of Westminster has sold father's beautiful picture[2] to Agnew, and Agnew to Sir Charles Tennant. I could not help writing to the Duke

[1] Arthur Lyttelton, Master of Selwyn College.
[2] Portrait of Mr. Gladstone by Millais.

thus in the first moment of my despair: 'Have you sold that picture? Oh, why did you not tell us first?' I hope I have not done wrong; really, I felt it so much it came like a shot."

The following letter describes a speech in Downing Street to the members for Durham, etc., on Lord Hartington's Irish record:

"*July* 8, 1887.

" Well, oh, dear dear, but it was grand—a quiet winding up and immense good expected to come from the speech, given to 700 picked delegates. Such enthusiasm, such attention, the voice never flagging. John Morley delighted, and, as Herbert writes, M.P.'s came back over the moon to House of Commons. Lord Granville was quite nervous, for the speech did require a fine hand, as to Lord Hartington especially. It was so Christian, allowing for differences on honest ground, yet showing up the dangers, viz. Hartington consenting to vote Tory, however much he disagreed; to keep the Liberals out. Never was there a better audience, seizing every point and entering so into the fun, *vide* Chamberlain's cushion and the sowing and reaping. I never read the Thanksgiving with more feeling. You will observe the *Times* even had forgotten for a moment its deadly rancour in admiration of the power and glorious ability. It was an evening to thrill over, an evening that made the life-blood tingle through one's veins. He is quite well. We dine at Dollis Hill, calling like Christians at Argyll Lodge on the way.

" Lady Acton seemed pleased at my going to her on way from Burnett's and Langhorne's. They have been very anxious about their son with typhoid."

" We are each of us still separately engaged in a death-grapple with *Robert Elsmere*," Mr. Gladstone wrote early in 1888 to his daughter, and on April 2: " By hard work I have finished my article[1]—rather stiff work."

At this time she wrote :

" We are deep in *Robert Elsmere*, one of the most extraordinary books. I am inclined (with Spencer) to think it may do good, but I have not finished volume three. It is not a book you can read fast—oh no, but I have a feeling father's review may be a corrective."

" 10 DOWNING STREET, *April* 1888.

" I have carefully digested the latter part of *Robert Elsmere*, and I am bound to say that I feel Catherine was wholly wrong in continuing her attendance at Elm Chapel—

[1] Review in the *Nineteenth Century*.

so very wrong that one stood amazed that, with the nobility of soul which she showed in the beginning of her life, she should fall so low in her mixing up of her religions. Yet I believe her faith in the Divinity of Our Lord was there; then you will say it was the more wrong she should go to the chapel as well as the church.

"Poor thing, her love for him clouded her understanding. The book, more than ever, leaves a bad taste in one's mouth. I have had quiet hours to digest the review [*Nineteenth Century*]—and to be very thankful for it."

AFTER GOING OVER TO SAIGHTON

"*April* 1888.

"The visit to dear Lady Grosvenor a success; the new husband [1] made a pleasant impression upon me—the snug family group quite like a novel, as after luncheon we went into the conservatory for coffee; picturesque, cosy, homelike, pretty young Pamela [2] playing, and singing to a guitar, roses hanging overhead and heliotrope. Enter two nurses, each with her baby; one from Eaton, the other Lady Grosvenor's. Of course I nursed each one; the Wyndham baby [3] such a beauty, four

[1] George Wyndham.
[2] Pamela Wyndham (Lady Glenconner).
[3] Percy Wyndham, killed in action September 1914.

months, sapphire eyes, hair dark brown; most beautiful the atmosphere, so unfine, happy, welcoming."

Here is a note from the Durdans, February 1889:

"At 6.30 we came to the Durdans, falling in with Rosebery and E. Hamilton at the station, and here we are, no one else, in deep snow. Father delights in the house and the books and the quiet; you could hear a pin drop. Curious to relate, Dr. Duncan declares Peggy's to be scarlet fever! Going on well, peeling all over, disinfecting cloths all hung about. Strange she could be ill ten days, supposed to be inflammation of the lungs, no throat, and that neither of the doctors should shoot [1] the complaint till the fever had gone and the peeling was high gee.[2] . . . It is good to talk with you, dear, whether depressed or not. . . .

"Post just going—your interesting letter I have only squinted at."

ON THE DEATH OF LADY ROSEBERY

"*November* 20, 1890.

"I have had the most touching letter from Lady Leconfield—the end was peace."

[1] *Glynnese Glossary*: to discover.
[2] *Ibid.*: in full fling.

Lady Rosebery's death took place on November 19, 1890. This was a great loss and sorrow to Mrs. Gladstone, for, quite apart from her deep affection and regard for Lord Rosebery, her friendship for his wife was of long standing. They understood and loved one another. In the following letter, very typical of the conflicting events and emotions of one short day, she tells her daughter of these contrasts, life and death jostling each other. In Berkeley Square the crowd outside the house, the solemnity and silence within—" How different a scene to the late gay parties." She dwells on the touching interview with Lord Rosebery and his boys—the masses of flowers round the coffin, the placing there of the white roses she carried in her hand. Mr. Gladstone accompanied Lord Rosebery to the funeral; she mentions how much it touched her that their father should ask her to stay with his younger children. In their schoolroom above, she knelt and prayed with them. From this house of mourning she went on to yet another smitten home. She continues :

"CARLTON GARDENS, *later.*

" I was greatly surprised at reading the Jewish Burial Service—so very fine (as far as it goes, I mean)—the chosen texts—it was read in Hebrew. Father had, after Lord

Rosebery, to throw earth upon the coffin. He stood close to him and his boys, and was greatly affected. Oh, Mary, when I think of the two scenes of yesterday—in poor Berkeley Square and afterwards at the Speaker's,[1] the sympathy that was wrung from my heart as the poor Speaker poured out his griefs.[2] Then the Ladies' Gallery and the sickening appearance of Parnell [3]—the astounding revelations—the mixture of ability and folly, the contradictions in that unfortunate man, the terrible throwing away of extraordinary gifts. . . . Professor Stuart has really been of great use—some call him fussy, and what does that mean but that he does not let the grass grow—that he sees when prompt action is important? I was struck by Herbert Paul—wise, judicious, cool-headed. Then there is father—calm, dignified, resolute, feeling the battle is but beginning, the Tories in the meanwhile clapping their hands."

"CANNES, *January* 15, 1892.

" I need not tell you the pang last evening brought in the tragic intelligence of Prince Eddy's death,[4] though I had been scolded for frightening myself. I was not really prepared; it seemed too dreadful to be true. Oh, darling

---
[1] Rt. Hon. Arthur Peel.   [2] Mrs. Peel's death-bed.
[3] The divorce proceedings.
[4] Eldest son of the Prince of Wales, died January 1892.

Princessy and the young wife to be. Galignani speaks of complications. I fear he caught cold at Count Gleichen's funeral. . . . The thought of dinner made me feel sick after such tidings. . . . Father wrote a very beautiful letter to the Prince of Wales, which I have copied hurriedly for you. I trust the reports of poor Princess being ill are exaggerated. All this frightens one as to Prince George."

After Mrs. Gladstone's return to England, she heard from the Princess's own lips the story of the illness and death of her beloved eldest boy. Very near the end, as she sat near his pillow, in his restlessness and delirium, he suddenly turned his head and looked at her. "*Who is with me?*" he said.

"*Our Lord Jesus Christ,*" was her answer. And from that moment quiet came to him, and the look in his eyes was of one who saw a vision.

"*February* 1892.

"I have finished Miss Benson's novel.[1] Helen and I rather agree as to its being very unequal. It rather jars me sometimes, the slang—and then I am jealous of goodness being made disagreeable; and don't you think there are exaggerations in Ruth's character? The

[1] *At Sundry Times and in Divers Manners*, by Mary Benson.

husband is not well drawn. Still, I agree with you—there are very beautiful bits, and much that shows great insight and great talent."

To Mr. Gladstone

"1893.

"... Hawarden all in sunshine. Dossie bewitching; sprang into my arms and actually kissed 'Master Pins,'[1] irrespective of beard.

"We must be patient with the Queen. By degrees she will gain courage to speak instead of only writing. As to the Opposition I cannot trust myself to speak, but Heaven will bless you, God grant, more and more."

"Hawarden, undated.

"Miss Eleanor Bellairs[2] tells a funny story of the Primrose League. One of their young maids went to a party given by the Primrose League, and in her own words:

"'Mrs. —— stood up and made a beautiful speech.'

"'What did she say?'

"'Oh, she said as 'ow we were to follow Gladstone. She said to us all: You know the story of Mary and the little lamb? Says

---

[1] George Armitstead, M.P.
[2] Her father was rector of Bolton Abbey, Yorkshire.

she, Gladstone's like Mary and we are like the little lamb. He puts a string round them and leads them wherever he likes! It was all so plain, it was—we have nothing to do but follow Gladstone.'

"Miss Bellairs declares that the poor young woman never discovered that the lady in question was labouring to warn them against Gladstone and the evil influence which made people follow him as the little lamb followed Mary."

There are countless letters dashed off in the intervals of each progress—for every journey, every voyage, became a progress more than royal, and each one seemed to beat the last in spontaneity and enthusiasm, people assembling even along the railway lines and in the stations where the train never paused. They begin with the historic visit to Newcastle in 1862—the newspapers of the day relate how the bells were rung, the guns thundered, 'the bands played, as the procession steamed majestically down the Tyne, ships flying their gayest flags, the river-banks black with thousands of people. Midlothian in 1879 and 1880 was possibly the climax, but the South Wales tour in 1887 was a marvellous experience, 60,000 working men sacrificing their day's wages and paying their own expenses to come to Swansea from all parts of Wales, for a touch of his hand or a glimpse of his face. It need hardly be told how she shared in these mighty demonstrations. Often she managed to save her husband by stretching out her own hand to be touched or grasped by the multitude. The summer of 1895 saw his last voyage. He and Mrs. Gladstone in the *Tantallon Castle* went as the guests of Sir Donald Currie to the opening of Kiel Harbour. No one ever foresaw more truly than he did the overwhelming conflagration that must, sooner or later, be the outcome of that great assembly of rival battleships, and of the piling up of armaments.

Here are two or three specimens of these letters:

" Yesterday was a day which must hold a place in the hearts and minds of thousands, long after the first enthralment has died down. I think the young will speak of it to their children, as they bless God for raising up one whose great gifts and energies could thus spend themselves on his country's good, heart and soul stirred by the one hope and desire to raise his fellow-creatures for the honour and glory of God. Towards the end it seemed as if all the energies of the man rose to their fullest strength—the voice more melodious and clear, and power seemed to be given him as the occasion demanded . . . it was the soul in him that spoke."

At Torquay in 1889 she speaks of " a procession three miles in length, we with our four horses at walking pace, enormous masses of people, imagine this place of places at its best, white-crested waves, the wealth of blossom and verdure, myriads of wild flowers. He was not so tired as I was at the end of the day, spite of his speeches and howling cheers in his very ear. At Dartmouth we had good sleep till four, when our yacht started for Falmouth. Though we roll, and the drawers, etc., fell about, no one was sick. I have just peeped at him; he is reading, and spoke to me with his happy, wicked look, so surprised at his own wellness."

"LLANHYDROCK HOUSE,[1] BODMIN, 1889.

" Looking back upon the last days of our progress, it is all a marvel to me, first of all his strength, his vigour of mind—the whole management of each speech with almost mathematical arrangement and yet such genius, adapting each to the circumstances of the place and people. The brain-power, the enthusiasm, the force, the pathos, and as yet I see no harm. Plymouth will be the most important day.

[1] The home of Lord and Lady Robartes.

To-morrow, after seeing something of this beautiful place, we are going to drive twenty miles to Lady Hayter's,[1] four horses to fly with us, and I hope a quiet evening. The Trelawneys are here, old good friends, and Freddy Leveson; such a house, great glorious galleries, such ceilings, such a gateway, such kindness."

[1] Tintagil.

CHAPTER V

LETTERS TO HER

SOMEONE has said that a man's character may be guessed from his books, and though there is truth in the idea, it would have been more true if the word correspondence had been substituted. Certain it is that in the case of Catherine Gladstone, the letters received by her bring to view attributes not generally recognised. They are lights that show up the different facets of a jewel. The letters here selected speak for themselves, but there is one aspect which, reading them as a whole, shines out above all others—her character as mother, not alone to her children, but to all sorts and conditions of men.

The art of letter-writing is not easy to define, but certainly one among its merits is the power to make small things live. Whose interest has not been more really quickened by Mrs. Carlyle's accounts of her domestic worries than by any of the letters written by her husband? To be really effective, letters must be spontaneous, not laborious. Mrs. Gladstone was alive to her finger-tips—her own letters were essentially human documents, and a reflection of them is to be found in the letters of her correspondents, only a very few of whom it is possible to mention in these pages.

First among them must be given two of the mass of letters written to her by her husband.

Absent from each other they never were, but for the imperative call of duty—any anxiety, physical or mental, of any of the members of their respective families. But both lived to the age of eighty-eight, so that the number of their letters to one another is considerable. The two following letters are chosen—the first on account of its deep personal nature—the other on account of its great historic interest.

In the first letter we recognise that under all the agitated surface of a life of turmoil and contention, "there flowed a deep, composing stream of faith that gave him, in face of a thousand buffets, the free mastery of all his resources of heart and brain."

It was written little more than four years after their marriage, and she evidently had failed to realise, in that short time, the imperative calls of public duty on his days and nights. She had evidently murmured at his prolonged absence and absorption, and she must have been pleading for some relaxation, for more time to be spent with wife and children; she must indeed have ventured to point out to him that here surely lay the first duty of a father and a husband.

"13 C.H.T.,
"*Sunday evening, January* 21, 1844.

". . . I am going to end this day of peace by a few words to show that what you said to me did not lightly pass away from my mind. There is a beautiful little sentence in the works of Charles Lamb concerning one who had been afflicted: 'He gave his heart to the purifier, and his will to the Sovereign Will of the Universe.'

"But there is a speech in the third Canto of the *Paradiso* of Dante, spoken by Piccarda, which is a rare gem: 'In la sua voluntade è nostra pace.' The words are few and simple, and yet they appear to me to have an inexpressible majesty of truth about them, to be almost as if they were spoken from the very mouth of God. It so happened that I first read that speech on a morning early in the year 1836, which was one of trial. I was profoundly impressed and profoundly sustained, almost absorbed, by these words. They cannot be too deeply graven upon the heart. In short, what we all want is that they should not come to us as an admonition from without, but as an instinct from within. They should not be adopted by effort, but they should be simply the habitual tone to which all tempers, affections, emotions. are set. In the Christian mood which ought never to be intermitted, the sense of this conviction should recur spontaneously, it should be the foundation of all mental thoughts and acts, and the measure to which the whole experience of life, inward and outward, is referred. The final state which we are to contemplate with hope, and to seek by discipline, is that in which our will shall be *one* with the will of God; shall live and move with it, even as the pulse of the blood in the extremities acts with the central movement of the heart. And this is to be obtained through a double process: first that of repressing the inclination of the will to act with reference to self as a centre; the second to cherish, exercise, and expand its new and heavenly power of acting according to the will of God, first perhaps by painful effort in great feebleness, but with continually augmenting regularity and force, until obedience become a necessity of second nature. . . .

"Resignation is too often conceived to be merely a submission. But it is less than the whole of the work of a Christian. Your full triumph, as far as that particular occasion of duty is concerned, will be to find that you not merely repress inward tendencies to murmur—but that you would not, if you could, alter what in any matter God has plainly willed. . . . Here is the great work of religion; here is the path through which sanctity is attained. And yet it is a path evidently to be traced in the course of our daily duties. Our duties can take care of themselves when God calls us away from any of them. . . . To be able to relinquish a duty on command shows a higher grace than to be able to give up a mere pleasure for a duty."

The other letter tells of the epoch-making speech delivered by Mr. Gladstone in reply to Mr. Disraeli's first Budget, December 1852.

"Like two of Sir Walter Scott's champions, these redoubtable antagonists gathered up all their force for the final struggle, and encountered each other in mid career. How rather equal than like, each side viewed the struggle of their chosen athletes, the fortunes of two parties marshalled in apparently equal array."[1]

"I have never gone through so exciting a passage of Parliamentary life," he wrote to Mrs. Gladstone on December 18, 1852. "I came home at seven, dined, read for a quarter

[1] *Times*, December 18, 1852.

of an hour, and actually contrived to sleep for another quarter of an hour. Disraeli rose at 10.20, and from that moment I was on tenter-hooks, except when his superlative acting and brilliant oratory absorbed me and made me quite *forget* that I had to follow him. He spoke till 1 a.m. His speech, on the whole, was grand, the most powerful I ever heard from him. At the same time it was disgraced by shameless personalities. When I heard his personalities I felt there was no choice but to go on. My great object was to show the Conservative party how their leader was hoodwinking them. The House has not, I think, been so excited for years—the power of his speech, the importance of the issue, the lateness of the hour were the causes. My brain was strung high, and has not yet got back to calm, but I slept well last night. Still the time is an anxious one, and I am very well and not unquiet. I am told Disraeli is much stung by what I said. I am very sorry it fell to me to say it. God knows I have no wish to give him pain; and really with my deep sense of his gifts, I would only pray they might be well used."

The *Times* writer contrasts the two speeches in this Homeric battle: "Mr. Disraeli's speech was in every respect worthy of his oratorical reputation. The retorts were pointed and bitter, the hits telling, the sarcasm keen, the arguments in many respects cogent, in all ingenious, in some convincing. The merits were counterbalanced by no less glaring defects of tone, temper, and feeling. In some passages invective was pushed to the limit of virulence, and in others, the coarser stimulants to laughter were very freely applied. Occasionally whole sentences were delivered with an artificial voice and a tone of studied and sardonic bitterness, most painful to the audience, and tending to diminish the effect of this great intellectual and physical effort. The speech of Mr. Gladstone was in marked contrast—pitched throughout in a high tone of moral feeling—the language was less studied, less ambitious—and though commencing in a tone of stern rebuke, it ended in words of the most pathetic expostulation. That power of persuasion which seems denied to his antagonist, Mr. Gladstone possesses in great perfection—and when he concluded the House might well feel proud of him, and of themselves."

The blow to protection and all its works resulted in the defeat of the Conservative Government, and Mr. Gladstone became Chancellor of the Exchequer for the first time.

This appears to have been the only occasion that Mrs. Gladstone was absent from her husband at a great crisis in the history of our times. In a letter written to her a few days later, Mr. Gladstone comments on the unexpected loss of temper shown by Lord Derby on his resignation of the Premiership: he contrasts it with what took place in the House of Commons. "Nothing," he wrote, "could be better in temper, feeling, and judgment than Disraeli's farewell." And thus the curtain fell after a victory which the *Times* described as "not merely a battle, but a war—not a reverse—but a conquest."

The earliest letter here printed, written by her cousin, Lady Delamere, to Catherine's mother, does not, strictly speaking, belong to her personal correspondence; but, owing no doubt to its historical interest, she carefully preserved it amongst her papers, and the same reason seems to justify its inclusion in the present volume. Written in the year before Waterloo, the letter gives a lively description of Blücher and Platof. The original is adorned with clever pen-and-ink sketches of the two generals.

FROM LADY DELAMERE [1] TO LADY GLYNNE

"*Sunday* [1814].

"MY DEAREST MARY,—I did not receive the little books which you were kind enough

[1] Mrs. Gladstone's cousin.

to send Hugh [1] three days ago, or I would sooner have written to thank you for remembering the little fellow. I am most happy to hear such good accounts of your Stephen, and trust that he is now quite recovered. I am so exceedingly hurried and bustled with all that is going on that I really have not a moment to spare, and what with going to see Emperors, Illuminations, Jugglers, and such like, and arranging dresses for the evening, I have hardly time for my *meals*. The other night I had a famous view of all these lions at Carlton House, where they all came the evening after their arrival. It was very fine, but rather alarming; however, perhaps you will like particulars. We arrived at ten, and found at the upper part of the first room a circle made carelessly with arm-chairs, into which we were in process of time ushered by the Lord Chamberlain and his White Wand. In the centre was the Queen, sitting on each side of her the Prince [2] and the Emperor,[3] and behind, the King of Prussia, his brothers, sons and nephews, the background being filled up with the Grand Duchess, Princesses, Duchess of York, Princess Charlotte, and the Prince of Orange. The *coup d'œil* was really very fine, and they looked like a royal family on the

[1] Lord Delamere, her first cousin.
[2] The Prince Regent. [3] Alexander of Russia.

LADY BRAYBROOKE AND LADY FORTESCUE
GRANDMOTHER AND GREAT-AUNT OF MRS. GLADSTONE
From a portrait at Dropmore

stage, which I think has a much better effect than when they walk about like us common individuals. The Queen and Prince spoke to every one, and some were introduced to the Emperor, but we thought it a flurry for nothing. When we got out of the circle we walked about in search of Blücher and Platof, who had each a little circle of their own, and the first is, as you see from the drawing annexed, a little square, stout old man with a very wild head of hair and immense whiskers covering his mouth entirely. He wore seven stars, infinite crosses, and from his neck hung a ribbon with the Prince's picture set in diamonds, which he gave him as soon as he set his foot in Carlton House. He is very old, but very *galant vis-à-vis des dames,* whom he is *particularly* fond of. As to Platof, he was in my opinion much the best worth seeing of any, as he looked like an inhabitant of the deserts, and the simplicity of his dress formed a wonderful contrast with the gold and silver which surrounded him. He wore a quite plain dark greatcoat, with only a little silver work on the collar and a silver sash, and black thick boots, having positively refused to wear shoes, never having had them on in his life. However, to make amends, the feather in his cap, which as you would see in my drawing is near half a yard long, was composed entirely of diamonds and emeralds most beautifully worked, which I was able to contemplate at my ease, as he gave me the cap in my own hand to look at. We stayed till about two, walking about quite at our ease, as there were only people enough to fill one room. . . ."

In June 1839 Mr. and Mrs. Gladstone were engaged to be married.

FROM THE RT. HON. THOMAS GRENVILLE

"CLEVELAND HOUSE, *June* 9, 1839.

"MY DEAREST CATHERINE,—I will not let one moment be lost in sincerely thanking you for tidings so sincerely gratifying to me. I am very fond of the great-nephew that you are giving to me, and very happy in the excellent husband that a bountiful Providence is giving to you.

"I knew Mr. Gladstone by character, and knew him to be one of the very few about whom there is but one voice; latterly I have had the pleasure of making his acquaintance, and am gratified beyond measure in thinking that your future happiness is committed to one so highly gifted in all that ensures it. Do not disregard these words as being mere congratulatory phrases, for I can well assure you that they are the honest expressions of the feelings of my heart, warmly interested about you and exulting in a marriage so promising of all that I could wish for you. . . .

"Say all the kindest from me on this happy occasion to your dear mother, and believe me always, dearest Catherine, your very affectionate old uncle,

"THOMAS GRENVILLE."

Charlotte Williams Wynn, Mrs. Gladstone's cousin, was a diarist of some note in her day, and had travelled extensively. She formed "close and lasting friendships" with Thomas Carlyle, Bunsen, and F. D. Maurice.

FROM CHARLOTTE WILLIAMS WYNN,

"*Monday* [1847]*.*

"MY DEAR CATHERINE,—Most heartily do I wish you joy upon the triumphant close to all your anxiety.[1]

"I must say that I never could be persuaded to doubt the result of the contest. Looking at the matter in its broadest view, it did not seem to me possible that a University could wilfully put away from her the man *with genius*, and clutch the man *without*.

"As others, however, had not as strong faith as I had on the subject, it must have been a very nervous time, and I long to hear that you

---

[1] Mr. Gladstone was elected Member of Parliament for Oxford University in August 1847.

are quite recovered. The last account of you was from your servant in Carlton Terrace, before I left town, upwards of a week ago.

"As far as Oxford, papa [1] and I travelled together, and there we separated, after I had passed two days more enjoyably than any two days I remember for years. Think of my never having seen Oxford before! You will be glad to hear that papa was not a bit the worse for the little exertion, and though at first he rather dreaded it, I think he enjoyed the whole thing, particularly his reception, which was very flattering. He then went on to Wales, and the election has passed off very prosperously.

"Of course, since my arrival here the only topic has been the unexpected putting forward of Cobden [2] and the sudden withdrawal of the Conservative Member. We were all at the Nomination on Saturday expecting that a Contest would ensue, and Lady Carlisle, who was here with her son, was in a state of fidget *beyond anything I ever saw*. However, after a wordy, trashy speech from Lord Morpeth (which had I been his mamma would have made me somewhat ashamed for him) the

---

[1] Charles Watkin Williams Wynn, M.P., in 1847, for Montgomeryshire.

[2] In the General Election of 1847 Cobden was returned for Stockport and for the West Riding of Yorkshire, where Lord Morpeth was the other member. Cobden decided to sit for the latter constituency, which he represented until 1857.

whole thing was quickly settled. Mr. B——
was, I fancy, literally frightened at the ghastly
show of white manufacturing hands held up
for Cobden, which looked like long lines of
breakers on a dark sea, so dense and unanimous was the crowd. He retired—and an
hour afterwards received an express from
Lord Fitzwilliam to say he would support
him with all the influence he had if he would
go to the Poll, but it was too late.

"I remain here another fortnight, and then
when Mary goes to the Lakes shall retrace my
steps, and pick up papa somewhere.

"He has just sent me Mr. Gladstone's
letter to him, which, though it answers in some
degree my question as to your health, will not
excuse you from writing when you are able
and inclined to do so.

"Adieu, give my love to your husband and
tell him how sincerely I congratulate him.—
Ever yours affy.,
"CHARLOTTE WILLIAMS WYNN."

FROM CAROLINE, LADY WENLOCK
"HAGLEY, Sunday, 1839.

"MY VERY DEAR PUSS,—Here I am in
dear Mary's[1] Palladian Palace; for it is
scarcely less! and more happy than I can
express, to see her so extremely comfortable.

[1] Lady Lyttelton.

She does really look like a bright gem in its proper casket, within these walls, and need not even yield the palm to her celebrated predecessor, the lovely Lucy, so famed in her *husband's lays*.[1] The house has been already described to you by Henry. I will only say therefore that it is as complete and as fine comparatively as either Stowe or Holkham, having nothing wrong about any part, and being exquisitely finished in the correct and chastened taste of its peculiar day. There is, too, such an atmosphere of high breeding about it that one cannot wish for modern furniture, or anything else, but to leave the things as they are—being the substantial result of many thoroughbred generations. They say the last Lord Lyttelton did wonders for the place in many ways, and all in the best taste. The modern plantations are beautifully managed, and there are no rabbits! I ought to call them single trees, perhaps, rather than anything else—and they are done with the most judicious eye.[2] We are going to town to-morrow, and then we return here to pass a few more days before we consider our visit made good. They have been so kind in forgiving its being disjointed, and to be sure 'L'homme

---

[1] *To the Memory of a Lady (Lucy Lyttelton) Lately Deceased: a Monody*, by George, first Baron Lyttelton. London, 1747.
[2] The beauties of Hagley have been described in Thomson's *Seasons*, 1744.

propose et Dieu dispose.' I am just returned from *such* a walk in the park, among (without exception) the finest trees I have ever seen—more like those at Wentworth than anywhere else, and with ten times more lovely grounds. I have enjoyed it beyond measure. They say there is every probability of the Queen's marrying, and that the Prince is very handsome. Miss Copley [1] told me the same thing—and a fresh report is current of Lady Cowper marrying Lord Palmerston,[2] provided Lady F. C. will accept Lord Emlyn; also that both the daughters much dislike the idea of Lady C.'s marriage. If you remain so late as the middle of November I fear you will find too many things to do before February, and we shall be cut short of our visit. Of all sensations here, I think the most lively for me is the idea of your dear mother [3] and what would have been her pride and delight in seeing this place. It is ever before my eyes. May it do me good, and remind me that every happiness below is meant to have its alloy, and may that alloy serve to wean us all from loving this world with an exclusive and engrossing love.—Your loving aunt, CAROLINE."

[1] Afterwards Countess Grey.
[2] Lord Palmerston married (December 1839) Lord Melbourne's sister, widow of Earl Cowper.
[3] Lady Glynne had a stroke in 1834, from which she only partially recovered.

While out shooting, Mr. Gladstone had blown off the forefinger of his left hand. In his Diary he noted, "I have hardly ever in my life had to endure serious bodily pain, and this was short."

From Cardinal Manning

"LAVINGTON, *September* 19, 1842.

"MY DEAR MRS. GLADSTONE,—I can in no way express the feeling with which I heard yesterday evening of the accident at Hawarden. But really I can hardly think of anything yet, but the great mercy that it was not of a more fearful kind. We ought to give God thanks very earnestly that he was so far preserved.

"I cannot help writing, though I am sure you do not need me to tell you how I have been thinking of you both.

"When you can find time to write me only a few words I shall be greatly obliged to you.

"Give my affectionate regards to him, and, believe me, ever your attached friend,

"HENRY E. MANNING."

From Samuel Rogers

"*October* 27, 1851.

"MY DEAR FRIEND,—Pray allow me to thank you in the fulness of my heart for your kind and beautiful letter.

"Happy should I be to contribute my mite and follow you in any little influence I may have elsewhere. There is a good angel [1] among us whose heart and hand are always open, but she is now, alas! at Vienna, and if she has not already contributed, I will not fail to send her an extract from your letter to me.

"Pray give my love to one and all under your roof, not forgetting Mr. Gladstone and a little lady I can never forget.—Yours most affectionately,   SAMUEL ROGERS.

"HAREWOOD HOUSE, BRIGHTON."

Acceptance of the Chancellorship of the Exchequer in 1853 vacated the Oxford seat and necessitated Mr. Gladstone's re-election to Parliament. He was opposed by a son of Mr. Perceval, son of the Prime Minister who was assassinated, and strong efforts, in which Archdeacon Denison took a leading part, were made to prevent his return on the ground of his association with the newly formed Liberal Government.

FROM SIR STAFFORD NORTHCOTE (LORD IDDESLEIGH)

State of the Poll at 1 o'clock

Gladstone 519
Perceval 453
                                  ——
                                   66

Close of the day's Poll

Gladstone 585
Perceval 498
                                  ——
                                   87

---

[1] Angela Burdett Coutts.

"*January* 1853.

"DEAR MRS. GLADSTONE,—I think we shall win by about 100, as far as one can venture to guess, but it is blind work. I do not, however, apprehend that there is the least real danger of actual defeat. We have several men who will come up rather than see us defeated.

"Lord Ashburton voted for us to-day—our second peer (Lord Saye and Sele was the other). MR. BENNETT [1] VOTED FOR PERCEVAL. The force of imagination can go no further.— Yours very faithfully and sincerely,

"STAFFORD H. NORTHCOTE.

"The Dean of Llandaff came here on his way to Madeira, for which he starts to-night, to vote for us."

FROM LORD LINCOLN (afterwards DUKE OF NEWCASTLE)

"WARREN'S HOTEL, *Saturday afternoon* [1849].

"MY DEAR MRS. GLADSTONE,—I have not the heart to call upon you to-day—to-morrow I hope to have slightly recovered from the sad and bitter feelings which your good, kind husband's letter has produced.

"None but those who after a long and pro-

---

[1] A former strong supporter. The final election figures were: Gladstone, 1022; Perceval, 898; majority, 124.

tracted mental suffering have allowed themselves to be buoyed up for a time by some new visionary hope can at all sympathise with me in all the sadness and depression which this renewed blow has occasioned. . . .

"If you will allow me I will call upon you after morning church to-morrow.—Believe me, my dear Mrs. Gladstone, LINCOLN.

"I assure you my own grief does not make me forget all the trouble and annoyance my dear friend is undergoing *for me*."[1]

FROM THE DUKE OF NEWCASTLE

"CLUMBER, *January* 31, 1853.

"MY DEAR MRS. GLADSTONE,—Your kindness to me and my children is really very great, and I cannot say how much I am obliged to you for the way in which you are now showing it.

"I really do not know what I could have done if it had not been for the way in which you have adopted them.—Ever yours most sincerely, NEWCASTLE."

Mrs. Gladstone mothered his children, both in her house in London and at Hawarden Castle, during a time of great trial.

Appointed Governor-General of India in 1856, Lord Canning found his path beset with

[1] See p. 71.

difficulties from the first. Not only did his first year of office witness trouble with Persia which resulted in war, but the intricate question of the Oudh settlement had also to be dealt with. His second year of office was marked by the infinitely more serious outbreak of the Indian Mutiny, which had been in progress for six months when the following letter was written.

From Lady Canning

"CALCUTTA, *August 7*, 1857.

"I have not written to you for an age, but I think I may as well prepare a short note for this mail. Not that I shall tell you *news*, but I think you will have thought of us so much in the terrible events of the last three months that you will like to hear of us. I think this dreadful war is so purely 'defensive' that I may count upon having Mr. Gladstone's sympathy with us, and his hearty support in giving all help from England. I am sure too he will see a mark of Providential interposition in the fact that the China Armament, of which he so much disapproved, is turned aside to such great service, and that Providence brings it within reach at the time all other resources are exhausted. All this is very striking. We have as yet only two of the China ships, and three-quarters of two admirable regiments turned back from the Straits. Lord Elgin promised to send all, but I fear his orders are not at Singapore yet for the rest, but I suppose all will come. We have to fight the Bengal army (all over Upper India and Bengal), all but about a third, which is either disarmed or quiet. Well affected can be said but of *very* few regiments, and we have but very few English regiments to fight with. Between this and Delhi at the outbreak there were but four, counting the whole of Oudh and the whole valley of the Ganges — 1000 miles. The exertions have done a great deal, but it is as anxious work as ever, and after the horrors of Cawnpore we are in the greatest anxiety that Lucknow may be saved, and we fervently hope that it is not too late. It holds out, and the assailants are short of ammunition. There are numbers of women and children in it, and to think of the long suspense of these poor things is really terrible — 1500 or 2000 men put to flight and beat 13,000, taking 12 guns. As General Havelock's fire has done this, we may trust it will be safely taken on the remainder of the march.

"Agra is believed to be safe and not as yet besieged; it was attacked and left. They have a very strong fort well supplied. Poor Lady Outram, who is shut up in it, writes in good heart to Sir James, and feels chiefly anxious about her son, who is skirmishing about in volunteer cavalry. Sir James has been in the house with us for a few days since he arrived from Bombay. He now goes on to take the command of the Dinapore Division, when he supersedes an old General Lloyd. This poor man is in very bad odour with every one for his sad mismanagement; instead of disarming three regiments he allowed them to escape, and the disturbances have taken fresh root, and now the flame rages in Bengal itself. I could tell you heart-breaking stories of sorrow and horrors to make your flesh creep, but you will have enough of it all in newspapers. We have been so struck at the actual happiness it has been to many people to find that their relations' names were in a list of deaths by *cholera* and wounds found at Cawnpore, with the date showing they were spared from the last horrible massacre.

"You can never imagine the surprise all this horrid revolt has caused here. I think perhaps all the more to those most used to India. The trust and confidence reposed in sepoys was so unbounded. They were so well treated, so prosperous, and so well behaved, and this time the murmurs arose on a question which seemed so easily explained, and the only grievance was one at once removed. Or rather it was so simple to show it had never existed, for no greased cartridges had ever been served out (only used a very short time in a school of musketry), one could not believe the delusion would be so industriously propagated with all the foolish stories about Lord Canning's pledge to the Queen and to Lord Palmerston.

"Now the Hindoos are quite aware of the tool the Mussulmans have made them, and I believe they have no great fancy for their old masters. The strange contrast of Lord John's drinking the health of the Princes of Oudh and Major Bird returning thanks when we have shut up the King, is almost amusing. The King, I believe, is quite a dupe of his ministers, but the Oudh Court and the emissaries of the King of Delhi are at the bottom of the whole, and the plot is evidently of long standing.

"If they could have been turned out of Delhi at once, the disaffection would never have spread as it did, but now it seems to have reached its limits in Upper India, and if Bombay and Madras keep quiet through the Mohammedan feasts of this month, I hope we may say we have seen the worst. Poor General Anson's death was a very great loss. I am sure he would quietly and firmly have done the very best service.

"Sir H. Barnard we have heard little about; he had a brilliant victory and repelled many attacks, and now the cholera has carried him off. The death of Sir H. Lawrence was most sad; his was a noble character in every possible way, and had done so well in those last times of great difficulty. Some few capital new men have come forth. Brigadier-General Neill you are sure to see praised in newspapers, and he deserves it; he is quite new, and comes from Madras as Colonel of an E.I.C. European regiment. We have often the whole population of Calcutta in a state of most abject panic, which must have the bad effect of ruining the natives' opinion of their own power. At last the 'Volunteers' were allowed both horse and foot, and we have enough English soldiers to guard against all sudden alarms. In the last three nights C. has allowed an English guard and now even our bodyguard has quietly given up its arms: we have really nobody to attack us. I cannot touch upon these topics without telling of all at too great length. Lord C. has kept well (excepting a few days) through all his anxiety and toil. I must say he looks upon it as calmly and coolly as possible.[1] The country must suffer greatly in every way; civilisation

---

[1] Lord Canning's calmness and clemency have been fully justified by history.

goes back full fifty years, for it is clear that the people had rather not have it and are not ready for it, and the number of burnt factories and sugar and indigo works and ruined merchants is very great. I believe the natives have taken alarm at the increase of Education, and whether secular or religious they do not much remark, for either undermines their superstitions and religion. Lord Ellenborough had better not have made that cut at Lord Canning; giving his weight to the foolish reports against him. I am sure Mr. Gladstone would know how very little he of all people would incline to interfere with liberty of conscience. We have not a notion to what subscriptions Lord E. alludes, for it happens that there are none to missions—only several school subscriptions to great and useful schools. I have got credit, I find, for 'doing a great deal' and visiting schools. The whole amount of my visits was one to each girls' school in Calcutta, five in number, and five to the school under Government for high caste girls for secular instruction, and this was wholly supported by Lord Dalhousie before I came. This was in ten minutes, so I can take little credit or blame to myself on this score; and this year I have done much less. We must look forward to a long spell of Calcutta, and it is a good thing that the climate does not deserve its bad character in my opinion. I have never had but one slight attack of fever, and I do not think it disagrees with Lord C. on the whole. The Talbots are the worst specimens, and he has gone on without moving to the hills, and I think the excitement is rather wholesome as far as health is concerned. I hope you are well and strong. My love to Mrs. Talbot when you meet. I shall leave a page to fill in, if good news comes before Saturday night. Remember me to Mr. Gladstone.—Yours very affectionately,

"C. CANNING.

"The *Shannon* is coming up the river with troops on board. A piece of most excellent news—whatever they may be. Lord Elgin must have sent her. Madras sepoys are come too, and believed to be trustworthy, but I am afraid they are very small by the side of our former magnificent Bengal regiments and may be disinclined to face them.

"*August* 8.—Who do you think is about to arrive and pay us a visit but Lord Elgin himself in the *Shannon*, commanded by William Peel.

"It will be very pleasant to see such well-known faces, but better still the 1700 soldiers they bring us, just when so much is wanted. We shall get on well now.

"Remember me to Mr. Gladstone. I dare say you will see Mrs. Herbert; wish her joy of her new babe for me, and tell her about us, for I do not write to her to-day, and I know she cares to hear. Mrs. Talbot and you are sure to see and talk over our troubles. I feel much happier again now; we start afresh with new force to save and relieve those, in jeopardy still."

On February 10, 1860, Mr. Gladstone introduced one of his greatest Budgets,[1] "the most arduous operation I ever had in Parliament." It upheld the French Treaty, reduced the taxation on certain articles of food, and was designed to repeal the Paper Duty, but the last proposal was rejected by the House of Lords, by whom, however, it had to be accepted in the following year.

From Sir James Graham

"Grosvenor Place,
"*February* 11, 1860.

"I had intended to have called on you this morning to inquire after my friend, and to offer you my cordial congratulations. Applause will follow in from every side; you know that none is more sincere than mine. I cannot leave home this morning: yet I should have

[1] In a five-hours' speech.

liked to have shaken the hand of Gladstone. He has saved his colleagues in spite of themselves. He omitted nothing. He said nothing which ought to have been omitted; and all in his own perfect manner. I remembered Peel. He is, I hope, in a better and happier world. Had he been alive how he would have triumphed in the completion of his own work by the ablest and most faithful of his followers!"

The Duke of Argyll's allusion in the letter which follows is somewhat obscure, but, as it was written on the day before the Budget speech of 1861, it probably refers to the measures taken by Mr. Gladstone to carry the repeal of the Paper Duty through the House of Lords. This he did by including all taxation proposals in one Money Bill, which had to be accepted or rejected in its entirety.

FROM THE DUKE OF ARGYLL

"CLIVEDEN,
"MAIDENHEAD, *April* 14, 1861.

"MY DEAR MRS. GLADSTONE,—I cannot help writing you one line to congratulate you on your husband's successful ingenuity on Saturday, which made me as happy as when I joined you at the Crystal Palace last year;

THE RT. HON. W. E. GLADSTONE
1858
From a portrait by Watts in the National Portrait Gallery

and at which I rejoiced all the more, that I think the proposal as it now stands is not only the best way out of a difficulty, but thoroughly right and sound in itself.

"I could not help being reminded of a saying of an old Scotch body to a friend of mine when he proposed something which she thought very ingenious: 'Eh! Wullie, Wullie, ye may dee for want o' breath, but ye winna dee for want o' wiles.'

"I expect him to have a great triumph both as regards the Past and Present."

In 1861 the Prince of Wales met for the first time, in Cologne Cathedral, Princess Alexandra of Denmark. Needless to say, he loved her at first sight. The announcement of the betrothal was received with no ordinary interest by the public at large, and the future Queen at once established that position in the hearts of the people which she has ever since maintained. Describing the first meeting between Queen Victoria and the bride, a lady-in-waiting wrote to Mrs. Gladstone at the time, "No one can fail to be struck with the ease, grace, dignity, and absence of self-consciousness of her manner and bearing, and sweet intelligent look. The Queen seemed to take her to her heart at once."

FROM THOMAS WOOLNER

"29 WELBECK STREET,
"*September* 14, 1863.

"DEAR MRS. GLADSTONE,—I sent a copy of the photograph of Tennyson which I mentioned to you, addressed to you at Penmaenmawr. If you agree with me that it is one of the best likenesses ever done and as good as a photograph can be, you will think it almost worthy the honour of being presented to Mr. Gladstone to adorn the Temple of Peace, taking into consideration the great admiration which he feels towards the original of the portrait.

"I am happy to tell you that the cast of the bust came out very well indeed, and I am now only waiting till it becomes dry before beginning it in marble. But one person yet has seen it who knows Mr. Gladstone's face, and he said that he thought it by far the best head that I had done. I find, on comparing it with others in my studio, that it looks much more powerful than any of the others, and I think, all things being weighed, that it is the most complete of them all.

"I cannot enough thank you for the thought and trouble you took to aid me in carrying out my work; and it is one of the pleasantest memories of my extremely pleasant visit to

Hawarden that I was so fortunate to please you in the aspect of Mr. Gladstone's character which I tried to represent."

FROM GENERAL GARIBALDI
"CLIVEDEN, 24 *Avril* 1864.

"MADAME GLADSTONE, — Permettez qu'en partant je vous remercie de tout mon cœur pour votre généreuse amabilité à mon égard.— Votre devoué,
"G. GARIBALDI."

FROM SIR STAFFORD NORTHCOTE (LORD IDDESLEIGH)
"18 DEVONSHIRE PLACE, W.
"*April* 28, 1865.

"DEAR MRS. GLADSTONE,—I am very glad to find that there is a prospect of some definite action with regard to the sick in workhouses. The recent disclosures are a great reproach to us, and I sincerely hope you may succeed in getting the reforms you mention adopted.

"I will not fail to attend when the question comes before Parliament, and I will speak to some of my friends who are likely to take an interest in it, and try to get a good attendance."

In 1868 Mr. Gladstone became Prime Minister for the first time. The Queen had written on December 1 asking him to undertake the formation of the new Government; and on December 4, the date of Lady Lyttelton's letter, he had, in an audience at Windsor, agreed to accept office. In his Diary he wrote : " I feel like a man with a burden under which he must fall and be crushed if he looks to the right or left or fails from any cause to concentrate mind and muscle upon his progress."

FROM THE DOWAGER LADY LYTTELTON

"*December 4*, 1868.

" DEAREST CATHERINE-PREMIERE, — So the crisis has arrived, and the plunge is taken. Well, I suppose I must congratulate you and your dear husband — to *you* it will be an anxiety the more on his account. May it be blessed to you both. I can express my wishes for him no better than by the first four verses of the 20th Psalm,[1] which struck me as just fit for my purpose this morning. Perhaps in the railroad carriage you may have time to read them. Don't *think* of answering — only forgive the trouble. I could not help it. — Yours affectionately,

" S. LYTTELTON."

[1] The psalm beginning, "The Lord hear thee in the day of trouble. . . ."

From Lady Palmerston

"Park Lane, *December* 22, 1868.

"I am unfortunate in having called on you twice without success—to-day and last week—and I leave town to-morrow. I wished very much to find you, and to have the opportunity of congratulating yourself and Mr. Gladstone on your brilliant prospects, and to express all my good wishes on this occasion.

"Mr. Gladstone has had the good fortune to be able to form a Government which gives a hope of long continuance, and I am very sorry that my son William Cowper was unable to join it. I am going to Broadlands for a few weeks, and I shall hope on my return to find you and Mr. Gladstone in great health and spirits."

From Bishop Samuel Wilberforce

"Winchester House,
"St. James's Square, S.W.,
"*March* 13, 1870.

"My dear Mrs. Gladstone,—I could not help feeling to-day, when I saw *him* kneeling in that rapt devoutness at the altar's rails, that, if there are bad signs abroad, there are to me hopeful ones. When could a powerful Prime Minister of England have been so seen since Burleigh's time in the reign of Elizabeth: except perhaps Aberdeen and Peel?

"You will let me hear about Thursday. The Lord Chancellor and the Clarendons dine, and will *all* look in after ten.—I am ever affectionately yours,

"S. WINTON."

The "Mr. Reid" whom Bishop Wilberforce speaks so highly of in the letter which follows, and who was at the time but twenty-four years of age, is now known as Lord Loreburn, and became Lord Chancellor thirty-six years after the prophecy was made.

FROM BISHOP WILBERFORCE

"*May* 6, 1870.

"Will you invite a Mr. Reid, a young man, son of a Sir J. Reid who was some functionary in the Ionian Islands. The young man was a very distinguished Balliol man: an Ireland scholar. He held a school inspectorship—is now reading for the Bar; and will be Lord Chancellor. He writes for the *Daily News*, and *worships* Gladstone. He is a friend of Reginald. You met him at Winchester House.

"If you will send me 'Yes' or any better invitation, I will act."

The Public Worship Regulation Bill was strongly opposed by Mr. Gladstone at every stage, and in his speech of July 9, to which Canon

Liddon refers, he gave notice of six resolutions which, in his opinion, furnished a more secure basis for legislation; but his party declined to follow his lead, and eventually the Bill became law. Although proceedings under it were taken against several members of the Ritualist party in the 'seventies, it gradually fell into disuse and is to-day a dead letter.

FROM CANON LIDDON

"SLIGO, *July* 18, 1874.

" I have just been reading a full report of Mr. Gladstone's speech on the second reading of the Public Worship Bill in the House of Commons.

" And I cannot help writing to you to beg you, when an opportunity *naturally* presents itself, to express to him my most sincere and heartfelt thanks for so noble and considerate a plea for reasonable liberty in the Services of the Church. I did not write to him before the debate, partly on account of your recent sorrow,[1] and because I felt sure that he would have anticipated a great deal more than I could possibly say. His speech will have won the hearts of thousands of clergymen. The other day I was at Derry, and spent an evening with the Bishop there—Dr. Alexander.

[1] Mrs. Gladstone's brother, Sir Stephen Glynne, died in June 1874.

Referring to the debate, which he had just been reading, he said: 'I could not forgive Mr. Gladstone for our Disestablishment; but I own this speech completely draws me again to him. It entirely disposes of the charge that he is influenced by political motives in these matters, as such a speech must have forfeited a great deal of influence with the rank and file of the Liberal party.' And if an Irish Bishop can voluntarily say as much as this, it is easy to imagine the feelings of those who are nearer home and more immediately interested.

"Even if the Bill should become law, such words will not be without effect in governing its administration, and in checking the mere unscrupulous exhibition of partisanship in the highest places of the Church, as well as in inducing some of our brethren to reconsider exaggerations, whether of language or practice, into which they may have been betrayed. In any case, justice, and still more generosity, are not to be met with every day in public life, and I, at least, learn to prize conspicuous examples of them more highly as I get older. . . .

"Dear Mrs. Gladstone, if I have ventured to say too much, and especially at a time of such heavy sorrow, you will forgive me. But I am not without hope that an assurance of the profound and affectionate gratitude which Mr. Gladstone has once more provoked in, I feel sure, thousands of hearts, may be a comfort to yourself."

From Queen Victoria

"Osborne, *July* 22, 1875.

"Dear Mrs. Gladstone,—I received with much pleasure your letter announcing to me your eldest son's engagement to Lord Blantyre's youngest daughter, and hasten to offer my sincerest good wishes to yourself and Mr. Gladstone. Pray also offer my congratulations to your son. I can easily understand how much pleased you must be to feel that your future daughter is the grandchild of the dear Duchess of Sutherland, my dear and valued friend, who was also grandmother to *my* son-in-law. I do not know Miss Gertrude Stuart, but have always heard her highly spoken of.

"Before concluding, let me say how glad I was that Mr. Gladstone appreciated Angele's beautiful pictures. I wished he could see those he has done for me of Louise, and some which are specially successful as likenesses and works of art. Repeating my good wishes, believe me always,—Yours affectionately,

"V.R.I.

"You will, I trust, let me know when the marriage is to take place."

FROM CARDINAL NEWMAN

"THE ORATORY,
"BIRMINGHAM, *July* 4, 1876.

"MY DEAR MRS. GLADSTONE,—I thank you and Mr. Gladstone very sincerely for your invitation to breakfast on the 6th.

"I shall rejoice to receive Mr. Gladstone's articles on Homer's Apollo and Athene,[1] which he is so good as to promise to send me, having already read with much interest some portion of his remarks on the Homeric mythology."

Tennyson and his son Hallam visited Hawarden in 1876, but before accepting the invitation the poet had made a bargain that he might be allowed to indulge in his beloved pipe in the security of his bedroom, smoking not being then much in practice at the Castle. With him, the poet brought his newly written historical drama *Harold*, his "Tragedy of Doom" as he called it. It seems to have impressed Mr. Gladstone, and in an article in the *Contemporary Review* (December, 1876) on the Eastern Question he quoted the lines:

"The voice of any people is the sword
 That guards them; or the sword that beats them down."

---

[1] "Homerology," *Contemporary Review*, March, April, and July 1876.

From Lord Tennyson

"FARINGFORD,
"FRESHWATER, *November* 12, 1876.

"MY DEAR MRS. GLADSTONE,—Here we are returned to our winter quarters—we retain golden memories of our visit to Hawarden, and your statesman, not like Diocletian among his cabbages, but among his oaks, axe in hand. Has he anything to say about my drama? If so, let him say it quickly before *Harold* passes into stereotype, and then burn or return the proofs.

"I am glad Hallam made a favourable impression—I do not think any man ever had a better son than I have in him.—Always yours,
"A. TENNYSON."

The letter which follows is undated, but probably refers to the personal attack made by Mr. Chaplin upon Mr. Gladstone during a debate on the Eastern Question in February 1877. Mr. Gladstone's reply, a mixture of sarcasm and light-hearted banter, has been described as one of the most effective and brilliant ever spontaneously delivered in the House of Commons.

FROM THE DUKE OF WESTMINSTER

"CLIVEDEN, MAIDENHEAD.

"DEAR MRS. GLADSTONE,—Here for the day. I had to leave before I could write a line on all the iniquities of last night. I never remembered so gross a personal attack, so prepared and in such bad taste. It elicited a wonderful instance in the crushing reply of marvellous power and readiness. It did one good to-day to hear the expressions of sympathy and of admiration.

"I hope Gladstone does not really mind this sort of wretched attacks, and that he takes them as a Newfoundland dog does the worrying of a terrier.

"After C——'s language at Lincoln, of which I made a note, I was not surprised at the edifying performance that followed.—Yours sincerely,

"WESTMINSTER.

"P.S.—Little Molly [1] was looking at a marble profile of Dante yesterday and asked, 'Is that Gladstone?' That was rather funny, wasn't it?

"Did you hear Rosebery's child's delightful remark that she 'couldn't make her mind sit down'?"

---

[1] Lady Mary Grosvenor, now Lady Mary Stanley.

When Sir Henry Acland visited Ruskin in 1878, he expressed the opinion that the attack of brain fever from which he was suffering could have only one of two possible results, recovery being out of the question. Happily these forebodings were not realised. Ruskin had visited Hawarden before and after this attack of brain fever with "his health better and no diminution of charm," as his host noted in his Diary.

From Sir Henry Acland

"BLETCHLEY, *March* 10, 1878.

"MY DEAR MRS. GLADSTONE,—I am on my way back from Ruskin, at Coniston, and having to halt here for the first train (I came by the night mail thus far) I must write to you and Mr. Gladstone. I write to you, I own, simply or in great part as a relief to pent-up feelings which either did not exist or had no expression while I was with him. For now his mind is utterly gone. He cannot be rightly said to know anyone. He *raves,* in the same clear voice and exquisite inflection of tone, the most unmeaning words—modulating them now with sweet tenderness, now with fierceness like a chained eagle—short, disconnected sentences, no one meaning anything, but beautiful to listen to for the mere sound, like the dashing of Niagara. It did not move me, though he would alternately strike at me and tenderly clasp my hands—once only giving almost certain sign of knowledge. To my question, ' Did you expect to see me by your bed ? ' he answered in the most pathetic tone : ' Yes, I expected you would come,' and then no more light any more.

"On the 12th of February he had sent the copy of his description of the Turner drawings to the press. The Preface ends with these words (one of Turner's first pictures ; his first picture with words of poetry attached—one of Coniston Fells) : ' Morning breaks as I write, along these Coniston Fells, and the level mists, motionless and grey beneath the rose of the moorlands, veil the lower woods and the sleeping village, and the long lawns by the lake-shore. Oh ! that some had told me in my youth, when all my heart seemed to be set on these colours and clouds, that appear for a little while, and then vanish away, how little my love of them would serve me, when the silence of lawn and wood in the dews of morning should be completed, and all my thoughts should be of those whom, by neither, I was to meet more.'

"A week after sending this to press, his mind began to fail, and on the 24th he was down with the violence of the brain fever.

"I have thus ended my sheet. As I look on

his intelligent life, I seem to see how physically he has been overwrought, and approaching slowly this grievous precipice. And, as I reflect, I seem to have seen or known no similar man. Nor now is he like any other; nor would any other be like him. The hours spent with him seem to have added a new and solemn act to the whole drama of life; and though I looked on almost stolidly at the time and quite unmoved, I look back with a certain holy, strange awe at the mystery of a human soul displayed on earth; the deep, pathetic mystery of every human life.

"It was repeated to me what Mr. Gladstone had said of Ruskin the other day at Grillon's. You know how I lately wished and thought about his going to you. I never saw him again after he yielded to my earnest entreaty to recall his refusal. And you have his last letter to me. I shall be back presently, God willing, at my daily work; may it be better done and more wisely and holily—and if I find I can yet help Ruskin, I shall go back again. There is a good, kind, sensible doctor near him, at Hawkshead. His old friend, Mr. Severn, has been with him too for the last ten days."

The General Election of 1880 resulted in Mr. Gladstone's return to the Premiership for the second time. The Midlothian Campaign had been a triumphal procession, and at no time has the country ever been raised to such a pitch of enthusiasm as was then witnessed. As a result, the Liberals swept the country.

From Lord Bryce

"7 Norfolk Square, W.,
"*December* 9, 1880.

"Dear Mrs. Gladstone,—Will you allow me to congratulate you on this wonderful campaign, and tell you, though you are sure to know it from a thousand sources already, what a feeling it has stirred in the breasts of the working men and the hearts of the humbler classes even here in London, where people are supposed to be least sympathetic and excitable? I have been usually two or three evenings every week in the Tower Hamlets canvassing, and so have been able to judge of the passionate interest with which these poor people have been following Mr. Gladstone's progress. One can't mention his name at a meeting without everybody springing to their feet and waving their hats. There is a warmer enthusiasm for him now here in the East of London than there ever was before, even in the election of 1868, and whatever the West End may say or think or write, I think the East End would hardly yield to Scotland or Wales in the depth and intensity of their attachment to his name. It is not so much a reaction towards Liberalism; it is what strikes one as better and finer even than political earnestness; it is loyalty and gratitude to a character and career which are their highest political ideal. Pardon me for troubling you with these lines. I trust that you and he are none the worse for so much fatigue and exposure."

FROM THE DUKE OF WESTMINSTER

"EATON, *Wednesday*, 1880.

"MY DEAR MRS. GLADSTONE,—One line, for *you* have no time for more, to add to the miles of congratulations that are your due from every ' airt.'

"How gloriously rewarded Gladstone must feel himself to be in the triumph of all that is right over all that has been *so* wrong.

"We shall win one seat here and very likely both, and take this Tory stronghold.

"How right and graceful of Leeds if, as they propose, they elect Herbert.—Yours very sincerely and triumphantly,

"WESTMINSTER.

"You saw that *Shaftesbury* too had been captured."

The tragedy of the Phœnix Park murders roused a thrill of horror through all classes of society. The Prince of Wales wrote to Mr. Gladstone expressing his deep emotion, and the Queen was no less moved. At Her Majesty's request Mrs. Gladstone sent a portrait of Lord Frederick Cavendish to Windsor.

From Queen Victoria

"WINDSOR CASTLE, *July* 18, 1882.

"DEAR MRS. GLADSTONE,—I return with many thanks the touching, sad, but most peaceful and beautiful portrait you have kindly allowed me to see. It must be very comforting for poor Lucy[1] to have it to look at. Was any cast taken to enable a bust to be made?

"I send you a photograph of myself taken in the dress I wore at Leopold's wedding. It is much liked. The veil and lace trimmings are the *same* I wore at my own wedding forty-two years ago."

Prince Leopold, Duke of Albany, died in March 1884. Mr. Gladstone was in bad health at the time and confined to his room.

From Archbishop Benson

"LAMBETH PALACE, *April* 4, 1884.

"MY DEAR MRS. GLADSTONE,—I have not troubled you with letters while the papers

[1] Lady Frederick Cavendish.

(happily accompanied almost daily with commentaries better than the text from those who know) have kept us informed of the slow, quiet repair which we hope is better and sounder than a sudden reinstatement. But to-day, when one's eyes almost ached not to see Mr. Gladstone in his stall at St. George's, I cannot help sending you one word, not meant to draw a moment's additional trouble from you, but to assure you how very beautiful and touching was the service, in which I am sure your hearts joined.

"The Queen was wonderfully composed and strong, though she looked as if she had wept sorely. No one can ever forget the intense look of the Prince of Wales, or the way in which he was rapt in the service, and his sudden kneeling down at the head of the grave when the *Kyrie eleison* began. When he sent for me afterwards he looked so pale, and as if thoughts other than of earthly sorrow were with him.

"The young Duchess was at a private little service yesterday in the memorial chapel,[1] the very image of strong resignation, as the Dean told me. And a young officer said that the little service before the body left the vessel yesterday was even more impressive than

[1] Twelve years later Archbishop Benson died in Hawarden church, when visiting Mr. and Mrs. Gladstone. See p. 192.

the wonderful beauty and power of to-day. Every one says the Foreign Ambassadors were greatly impressed.

"In London even poor cabmen had crape on their whips in little bows. Surely England has not done with loyal love yet. Mr. Gladstone would have so entered into the piety and strength and *hope* of the scene to-day. Please no answer, I know how busy you are.

"With sincere hopes that every day and hour is strengthening Mr. Gladstone, and that you are well.—Sincerely yours ever,

"EDW. CANTUAR."

FROM KING EDWARD VII. WHEN PRINCE OF WALES

"MARLBOROUGH HOUSE, *April 7,* 1884.

"MY DEAR MRS. GLADSTONE,—Your kind letter which reached me to-day has deeply touched me, and I beg you and Mr. Gladstone to accept my sincerest thanks for your sympathy in the blow we have sustained. You have known us all since our childhood, and I felt sure would feel for and with us at the sudden death of our poor brother.

"If his life had been spared, he had a brilliant career before him . . . it is not for us to murmur.

"The Queen and my sister-in-law are bearing up as well as can be expected in their grief.

" With kind regards to Mr. Gladstone, who I trust is now quite himself."

From the Duke of Westminster

"CLIVEDEN, *May* 8, 1884.

" I wonder whether we might ask Gladstone to confer a distinguished honour on our youngest son by consenting to become his godfather ? We have the less hesitation in making this proposal, as we do not think it will give him much additional work, his coadjutors being Mary Cobham and Alfred Lyttelton,[1] ready to take all the work on to themselves. . . ."

This was Hugh Grosvenor, who lost his life in the Great War.

Holman Hunt spent practically ten years working on "The Triumph of the Innocents," of which there are two pictures, at Liverpool and Birmingham.

From Holman Hunt

"DRAYCOTT LODGE,
"FULHAM, *August* 1884.

" DEAR MRS. GLADSTONE,—I trust that you will not allow the request that I venture to make in this note, to hamper you in your many serious duties in the slightest degree, unless,

[1] Died July 1913.

with the wonderful power Mr. Gladstone has of relieving his mind from his heavy responsibilities, you think that the honour of a visit from him to my studio would be a wholesome and practicable relaxation.

"The picture, which it would be a great gratification to me to show both to you and to him, is one that I painted in Jerusalem some seven years since, but owing to the canvas being bad I was unable to bring the work to a conclusion without repeating it on another canvas, which has been a very trying task. It is now so nearly finished that it would be a disappointment to me to put off till your return to town this application, which I will confess I have kept in reserve as one of the pleasures to be earned by bringing my task to an end. The picture is an imaginary incident of the flight into Egypt, and it will be entitled 'The Triumph of the Holy Innocents.'

"I will gladly be at my studio any time on Saturday that you might be able to appoint."

The news of General Gordon's death was received in England on February 5, 1885, and on February 23, Sir Stafford Northcote moved a vote of censure on the Government. The final debate took place on February 27, and the division was taken at four o'clock on the morning of the 28th. The result was a narrow majority of fourteen for the Government.

From G. W. E. Russell

"House of Commons, *February* 27, 1885.

"My dear Mrs. Gladstone,—I fear you must be feeling sad and anxious about to-night. And, though I can do no good, I feel impelled to write you one line of true and loyal sympathy.

"Even if the worst happens, it will only be because Mr. Gladstone preferred duty to inclination, and stayed on when he might have gone out in a blaze of triumph. His fame is assured for all time, and no passing reverses can affect it.

"Never, I think, were you so encompassed with the love and trust of his real followers: and I personally should be the basest of the base if I did not, at this dispiriting moment, make a special acknowledgment of my gratitude and veneration."

The Afghan boundary dispute in the early part of 1885 occasioned grave fears of a war with Russia, but in May Mr. Gladstone was able to announce that a settlement had been arrived at.

From Sir Arthur Gordon (Lord Stanmore)

"Queen's Cottage,
"Onwara Eliya, 18/3/'85.

"My dear Mrs. Gladstone,—I began our *Pembroke Castle* cruise positively by actually *disliking* Miss Tennant.[1] I ended it, liking her very much and thinking highly of her. I am *really* growing old now, and am in feelings much older than my fifty-five years would warrant, for I have from my youth lived entirely with people older than myself, and made most of my more intimate friends among them. I have consequently a liking for *les manières d'autrefois*, which is not too often gratified nowadays. I must say I think well-bred women thirty or forty years ago had quieter, more refined and really polished ways than the young women of the present day can boast of, and were in consequence all the more agreeable to live with.

"I heard with much regret of Sir Robert Phillimore's death. He had not of late been so much or so closely associated with you as

---

[1] Miss Laura Tennant, afterwards Mrs. Alfred Lyttelton. The *Pembroke Castle* trip was taken by Mr. and Mrs. Gladstone in 1883; Sir Donald Currie was host, and Tennyson was one of the guests. In Copenhagen harbour Mrs. Gladstone was hostess to the Emperor and Empress of Russia, the King and Queen of Greece, the King and Queen of Denmark, the Princess of Wales, and many others. See *Some Hawarden Letters*.

was the case some years ago, but he was still one of the most true and faithful personal friends of Mr. Gladstone. I see an early dissolution spoken of. Aberdeen is to have two members. I wonder if they would take me as one?

"What crowds of events in the political world and what important and exciting ones! I shall lose something of my faith if it be possible that a war should result from the discussions with Russia—discussions which appear to me to be eminently of a nature for settlement by amicable negotiation. But on the whole, such a result seems to me to be impossible, for there is not sufficient reason for it. I do not forget, however, that the Crimean War seemed equally impossible, and that Mr. Gladstone cannot be more averse to war than my father[1] was. But there is this enormous difference in the situation—that Mr. Gladstone has no party intriguings against him in his own Cabinet, and that the negotiations are directly carried on between two Powers only, instead of indirectly and with half a dozen, as in 1854. This is all in favour of a peaceful issue.

"Though we are in the tropics, it is quite *cold* up here—frost at nights—fires in all our rooms—and a garden before the house with

[1] Lord Aberdeen, Prime Minister in 1854.

none but English flowers in it.—I remain, yours very affectionately,

"A. GORDON."

On her daughter's dangerous illness.

FROM G. W. E. RUSSELL

"WOBURN, *November* 4, 1886.

"MY DEAR MRS. GLADSTONE, — Lady Stepney's letter just received has caused us such joy that my father desires me to write at once, on his behalf as well as my own, to say how very thankful and happy we are, for your daughter's sake and for yours.

"There is no happiness on earth like the escape from fear, and God's mercy seems to shine more brightly when one has just emerged from a cloud.

"That you have been allowed so to emerge, and again to feel and see the light, is indeed an unspeakable mercy."

The split which occurred in the Liberal Party over Home Rule is a matter of history. Some of Mr. Gladstone's followers, like the Duke of Argyll and the Duke of Westminster, expressed their dissent from the new policy in various ways, but through all their attachment to Mr. and Mrs. Gladstone was maintained and their admiration undiminished.

From John Bright

"Euston Hotel, *June* 1, '86.

"Dear Mrs. Gladstone,—Your invitation is very kind, and I wish I could freely accept it; but at this moment, when I am driven into serious, but I hope only temporary, opposition to Mr. Gladstone in connection with his unfortunate Irish policy, I feel as though my company at your table could not be as pleasant to you or as satisfactory to myself as heretofore. You will see that I write frankly, explaining precisely why I will ask you to excuse and forgive me if I do not join you at dinner this evening.

"I cannot tell you how grieved I am at the crisis at which we have arrived, but judgment and conscience must rule rather than personal preferences. As for myself, if you cannot approve, I may hope that you will be able to forgive.—Believe me, very sincerely yours,

"John Bright."

The following letter refers to the tragic death of the Duchess of Argyll ten years earlier. She was taken suddenly ill at Lord Frederick Cavendish's house in Carlton Terrace, as Mr. Gladstone was handing her in to dinner. He carried her into the study, her sons and daughters were summoned, and she died the same evening in the arms of Mrs. Gladstone (May 25, 1878).

From the Duke of Argyll

"*July* 29, 1888,
"Argyll Lodge, Kensington.

"My dear Mrs. Gladstone,—I received your kind letter on Friday just as I was starting for Tennyson, and I could not write whilst there.

"Pray be sure that I can never dislike anything that you can ever say to me. The last sight I had of my dear one was in your arms, and I think of you, as of Her, as " very woman of very woman," as the great poet wrote of Her to me.

"But there is one thing I am not sure that you quite see—or at least fully estimate.

"'The Doctrine of the Two Spheres' is *generally* easy. But it becomes more difficult in practice when differences become fundamental with one who is not only a leader, but the *only* leader whose teaching is of any power.

"He can fire at us as a nameless group. We can't do this. His words and arguments are the *only* ones worth considering. We can argue with him alone.

"The alternative is to speak *at* him: or to speak *of* him.

"I hate the first—the second is always the

most respectful, but it sounds *more* personal. This really can't be helped.

"Pray also recollect how deeply this difference cuts into life. Poor Leinster died of nothing else. He died of a broken heart—on the Irish question. He was a devoted Gladstonian up to the Home Rule move, was quite angry with me on the Land Question. But the last move killed him. He saw the break up of all he had loved and lived for—he and his, for many generations.

"Such things can't be helped—in great revolutions. But if the Revolution be not certainly for the better, they are sacrifices which embitter—and are uncompensated to those who stand in former convictions.

"How very sad Evey Ailsa's[1] death! She was a very angel of goodness—therefore we need not grieve.

"I found Tennyson weak physically, but writing new poems as full of force and of pathos and beauty as ever.—Yours affectionately,
ARGYLL."

FROM THE DUKE OF WESTMINSTER

"EATON, *June* 27, 1892.

"MY DEAR MRS. GLADSTONE,—I have only just heard of this disgraceful act[2] by a dis-

[1] Lady Ailsa, his niece, sister of the Hon. Mrs. W. H. Gladstone.
[2] A woman in the crowd had thrown a missile which hit Mr. Gladstone in the eye.

graceful Chester woman, and I lament it greatly, and only hope that the annoyance may not have been felt much by Gladstone and yourself.

"It will have excited the disgust and indignation of *all* parties.—Yours under all circumstances, always affectionately,

"WESTMINSTER.

"No answer!"

Probably the most notable of Mr. Gladstone's speeches delivered outside the House of Commons was that made at Bingley Hall, Birmingham, in 1888, before an audience of some 18,000 people. Public excitement was at fever heat, and probably the only person in Birmingham who remained calm was Mr. Gladstone himself, then seventy-eight years of age. Indeed, it is remembered that on the day of the meeting, when the whole household with whom Mr. and Mrs. Gladstone were staying was filled with apprehension and excitement at the magnitude of the task before him, the chief actor was so deep in a Homeric discussion, that it was with difficulty he was induced to take his seat in the carriage which was waiting to convey him to Bingley Hall. Lord Morley has written a vivid description of the meeting and of the scene at the close—

"absolutely indescribable and incomparable, overwhelming like the sea."

FROM ONE OF HIS COLLEAGUES

"*November* 11, '88.

"MY DEAR MRS. GLADSTONE,—I had to leave Bingley Hall as soon as Mr. Gladstone sat down, for I was pressed to catch a train. Since then I have hardly put pen to paper, and have scarcely thought of anything else.

"He has beaten his record: his own record! There has been nothing like it. I am convinced from my own observations, and from casual words with odds and ends of people I met on railway platforms, that his noble speech was heard *all* through by 18,000 people. He shames the young, and is the despair of the old.

"I envy you more than him. Our eyes sympathised though we could not speak. I feel privileged to take something of the same sort of pride that his family takes in these performances. I could indeed have waited as far as my train was concerned, but I wished the evening to close for me with that splendid recollection.

"I am grateful to him personally for the stimulating idea of that august scene, which must have been a high incentive to every person present, however humble, who was interested in politics; and on behalf of the party, for an episode which places it in a new light of enthusiasm.—God bless you and him."

From J. T. Delane, Editor of the *Times*

"10 Serjeant's Inn, *June* 8.

"Dear Mrs. Gladstone,—When the Prime Minister on Wednesday last was good enough to ask me to dine with you on Thursday next I listened in, I hope, becoming wonder, that one, who knew so much, should not know that Thursday next is Cup Day at Ascot.

"He promised me a card, and when none came I hoped it was I and not he who had mistaken the day.

"Your note 'to remind' has dispelled the fond illusion, and I feel as Dr. Manning might feel if he had accepted an invitation to a Ball on Good Friday.

"Pray then intercede for me. I have a large party in my house at Ascot for the Races. I expect at least a hundred people, and most of your colleagues, to lunch there on Thursday. I had some hope that you yourself and Miss Gladstone might possibly honour me with your presence, and now I find myself partly engaged to dine with you in London.

"Pray allow me to defer the honour to

some other occasion, and forgive the rash assent of, yours very faithfully,

"JNO. T. DELANE."

The laconic answer of Tennyson to an invitation to breakfast.

FROM LORD TENNYSON

(Undated.)

"MY DEAR MRS. GLADSTONE,—I am sorry that we cannot come to-morrow, so is she.— Ever yours, A. TENNYSON."

What would the writer of the following letter have had to say about present-day fashions?

FROM DR. PUSEY

"CHALE, I. OF WIGHT,
"*Easter Tuesday*, 1870.

"MY DEAR MRS. GLADSTONE,—My dear friend, your husband, tells me that he has shown you the part of my letter which relates to the dress of the upper class of society, and that if I had anything to suggest you would be glad to speak with me, whenever I should be in town.

"As I hear, there are two classes of evil:

"1. The extravagance of dress.
"2. Its character.

"The first has its special evil both in preventing marriage (as so many young men cannot afford to marry such wives) and its horrible evils in consequence of young wives not daring to bring their bills to their husbands. This I have been told by married women, not by those who were guilty.

"2. The indecency. And this, as far as I hear, is more inexcusable in the young or middle-aged married women, because in them it can hardly be to please their husbands, except so far as a vain or foolish husband from time to time likes his wife to be an object of admiration even at the cost of propriety of dress. I have heard of such a case, when the wife was evil spoken of because the vain husband liked her to appear in this undress and surrounded her with the society of men, probably like himself.

"The second will be more easily withstood than the first. For a modest dress is really more becoming and more attractive than the immodest — I mean as far as attractiveness is a lawful object with mothers for their daughters. What any men who are worth having for husbands are really attracted by is simplicity and reality. I have known cases when persons without any beauty or much sense have been attractive, simply by their freshness and simplicity.

"The difficulty seems to be to persuade the

young women themselves before they have unlearnt the simplicity which, if unlearnt, can only be recovered by the grace of God.

"Yet I cannot but think that something might be done to check beginnings. Why should fashion be all in the wrong direction? Why should dressmakers have this autocracy? Or if they have it, why should their influence be on the wrong side? God has made His own work more beautiful than we can unmake it, and it is best set off by that which is becoming, *i.e.* suited to it.

"People have learned the power of union and adopt it as far as they can. Why should not something of this sort be done for God? We have plenty of associations for the poor. Why should not the good rich associate themselves for the protection of our young women, the mothers of the future aristocracy of England, that our young English girls might become again what they were in the days of your youth? Thus if a certain number of ladies, into whose houses mothers would wish to introduce their daughters, were, in issuing their cards for an evening party, to put (in French for the servants' sakes) something to the effect, 'It is required that ladies should not come in very low dress,' or the like, I should think a counter-tide of fashion might set in.

"However, you, who live in society, can

understand how everything is to be done for it, better than I who live out of it. But I feel sure that something could be done if those who can influence it do not look upon it as a hopeless evil, and so let the flood sweep on which is, one fears, sweeping so many to perdition.

"I wish also something could be done as to not inviting those persons whom people court also for their rank, but of whom charity itself can think no present good, but can only hope that they may be converted.

"Of course there will be obloquy and ridicule; nothing good is ever done which is not spoken against. But you will have people's consciences, their better feelings, their better selves, and God on your side, in setting yourself against this tide of evils; and you will find, I doubt not, as we did, when we began the *Tracts for the Times*, that many will range themselves on the right side as soon as a decided stand is made, who before stood loitering about, choosing neither. God prosper you.—Yours very faithfully,

"E. B. PUSEY."

The visit to Italy foreshadowed in the next letter duly took place, Mr. and Mrs. Gladstone staying with Lord Rendel at Naples, and there Lord Dufferin visited them. "I went," he afterwards told their daughter, "thinking I could give Mr. Gladstone valuable information concerning Egypt and India, but I discovered he knew much more about them than I did."

From Lord Dufferin

"Viceroy's Camp, Lahore,
"November 16, '88.

"My dear Mrs. Gladstone,—I had such a nice letter from Mr. Gladstone, and now you have been good enough also to write to me, which is very like old times.

"And now about Rome. I cannot conceive any circumstances in which you and Mr. Gladstone would not be welcome at the Embassy, or in which I could not contrive somehow to make you comfortable; but I must admit that next January would be a less propitious date than I could desire, for the simple reason that we do not ourselves get to Rome until the third or fourth of that month, and that the house is described as being so dilapidated and destitute of furniture that my wife and children, after staying for a few days, as at present arranged, in a hotel, go straight on to England, leaving me as a bachelor to do the best I can for myself until the workmen, painters and upholsterers have put the place in order. But, in spite of this unpromising state of things, it would be such a pleasure to me to have you and Mr. Gladstone as my guests, if you would accept my bachelor hospitality, that I would ransack all the palaces of the Roman Princes to make you comfortable; but common honesty has driven me to tell you the exact truth, so that I may not lure you into uncomfortable lodgings under false pretences.

I send you a very modest retrospect of my four years' work in India, which perhaps Mr. Gladstone might like to glance over. I think he will find that my Government has done more than is generally known or supposed. Nobody but the few experts who have been behind the scenes understand what a difficult time I have had in India, and how many dangerous problems I have had to deal with. The fall in silver alone was enough to have upset the coach, and scarcely six months passed without some new trouble developing itself, but for all that I shall hand over India to Lord Lansdowne without a cloud on the horizon, and what is still more satisfactory, if only silver does not take another bad turn, in a state of financial equilibrium, and that in spite of Burmah, Afghanistan, Thibet, and the Black Mountain.

"With my wife's kindest regards, believe me, dear Mrs. Gladstone, yours sincerely,

"DUFFERIN AND AVA."

A FAMILY GROUP AT HAWARDEN
1894

IN THE BACK ROW, READING FROM LEFT TO RIGHT, ARE MR. AND MRS. S. E. GLADSTONE, MRS. AND MR. H. DREW, LORD GLADSTONE, MISS HELEN GLADSTONE. THE BOY ON MR. GLADSTONE'S KNEE IS STEPHEN DEINIOL GLADSTONE

Mr. and Mrs. Gladstone celebrated the fiftieth anniversary of their wedding in 1889.

From Cardinal Manning

"Archbishop's House,
"Westminster, S.W., *July* 23, '89.

"My dear Mrs. Gladstone,—The last time we met you said, 'I do not forget old days,' and truly I can say so too.

"Therefore in the midst of all who will be congratulating you on the fiftieth anniversary of your home life I cannot be silent.

"I have watched you both out on the sea of public tumults from my quiet shore. You know how nearly I have agreed in William's political career: especially in his Irish policy of the last twenty years. And I have seen also your works of charity for the people, in which, as you know, I heartily share with you.

"There are few who keep such a Jubilee as yours: and how few of our old friends and companions now survive.

"We have had a long climb up these eighty steps, for even you are not far behind: and I hope we shall not 'break the pitcher at the fountain.' I wonder at your activity and endurance of weather.

"May every blessing be with you both to the end.—Believe me, always yours affectionately,

"Henry E. Card. Manning."

From the Empress Frederick

"Villa Zirio,
"*February* 8, 1888.

"Dear Mrs. Gladstone,—Pray accept my best thanks for your kind letter expressing so many wishes for the Crown Prince's recovery from this trying and protracted illness. We trust and hope they may all be fulfilled. The outlook is no longer as gloomy for us as it was in November, and this is a great comfort for which we are truly thankful.

"The kind sympathy of all friends in England is very gratifying to me.—Ever yours,
"Victoria,
"Crown Princess of Germany and Prussia and Princess Royal."

In 1890 the Parnell Divorce Case shattered for the time all hopes of an Irish settlement. Ever ready to take as its motto the dictum of Flaubert that "Nothing succeeds like excess," the Irish party was rent in twain and the air was filled with recriminations between Parnellites and anti-Parnellites. On the ground that he had helped to depose their leader, some of the former were not slow to vilify Mr. Gladstone.

FROM PIERCE MAHONY[1] (who supported Parnell)

"HOUSE OF COMMONS LIBRARY,
"*December 8*, '90.

"DEAR MRS. GLADSTONE,—I take the liberty of expressing to you the great sorrow it gives me to appear even for a time to be acting in opposition to Mr. Gladstone. In the course of the last ten days expressions have been used, in moments of great excitement and passion, regarding Mr. Gladstone, which have given me great pain. Whatever may occur in the future, I think that no expression will ever fall from my lips in any way inconsistent with the deepest respect for and gratitude to Mr. Gladstone. The kindness you have shown to me makes me hope that you will excuse me for troubling you with this letter.—Believe me, dear Mrs. Gladstone, yours sincerely,

"PIERCE MAHONY."

FROM QUEEN VICTORIA

"WINDSOR CASTLE, *May 7*, 1893.

"DEAR MRS. GLADSTONE,—Accept my best thanks for your very kind letter and congratulations on the betrothal of my dear grandson, George, with Princess Victoria Mary

[1] Now The O'Mahony.

of Teck, which gives me great pleasure, and which I trust will be the beginning of a long life of happiness to themselves, and be a blessing to their family and to the country at large.

"It is indeed a very long time that I have known you. At York in '85 I saw the two very beautiful Miss Glynnes and have not forgotten it. How much of weal and woe has happened since that time."

From G. F. Watts

"Little Holland House,
"Kensington, W.,
"*August* 4, 1893.

"Dear Mrs. Gladstone,—My wife very earnestly desires to have the honour, and she is worthy of it, of shaking hands once in her life with Mr. Gladstone. Could this be managed without intrusion upon time and attention so valuable? I also should like to have the same honour once more.—Very sincerely yours, G. F. Watts."

The horror of a tragedy still fresh in the minds of every one becomes still more poignant when one glances back to the time when all was bright and the future seemed filled with every augury of happiness. Writing to Mrs.

Gladstone in May 1894, Queen Alexandra said: "Thank you a thousand times for your very kind letter of congratulation on the engagement of my charming nephew, the Cesarevitch, to Alix of Hesse, dear Alice's youngest daughter. They both seem very happy, and I do hope that this union will be for their mutual blessing and for the welfare of our country, as we consider her half English, as well as for Russia, the land of her adoption."

From Margot Tennant

"Cold Overton, Oakham,
"*March* 1894.

"Dearest Aunty Pussy,—I was much touched by your message to Mr. Asquith.[1]

"I dare say I was a little out of spirits that night at the Campbell-Bannermans', and I thought you were lecturing me too severely, but I am sure you know I value all you say. I feel so deeply your present sorrow of retiring from so long and beautiful a public life; it will be a lasting example to me in my humbler future to remember your courage and devotion. God bless you and your dear husband.— I am, with all my faults, yours lovingly,

"Margot Tennant."

---

[1] The Rt. Hon. H. H. Asquith married Miss Margot Tennant in May 1894.

FROM SIR WILLIAM RICHMOND

"HAMMERSMITH, *April* 29, 1896.

"MY DEAR MRS. GLADSTONE,—I thank you for your kind and affectionate letter. We all, one and all of us, are delighted that my father's drawing has given you pleasure.

"Alas, youth only comes once in a lifetime, and whatever in after life recalls it by memories is very sweet and full of consolation.

"I have lately been reading and sorting out old letters of thirty years ago, with a mixture of pleasure and pain, but the pleasure on the whole predominates, by the memory of affection and love which are not dead but only sleep.

"If souls are permitted to meet in another world, how precious will be the intercourse sweetened and purified by separation!—Yours, dear Mrs. Gladstone, affectionately,

"W. B. RICHMOND."

When on a visit to Hawarden in 1896 Archbishop Benson died suddenly whilst attending service in the church.

FROM THE DUKE OF ARGYLL

"INVERARAY, ARGYLLSHIRE,
"*October* 12, 1896.

"MY DEAR MRS. GLADSTONE,—One line only to say how much we are all shocked and grieved for you all in this sad tragedy at Hawarden. It recalls only too vividly another link[1] in which you were a ministering angel indeed.— Yours affectionately, ARGYLL.

"Archbishop Benson was so kind to my son Walter when at Wellington College."

The following letter was written by Li Hung Chang after visiting Hawarden in August 1896:

"PEKING, *November* 2, 1896.

"DEAR MRS. GLADSTONE,—Your valuable autograph letter of the 3rd September gives me great pleasure.

"I arrived in Peking on the 20th ult., and had, on the following day, a long audience with the Emperor and his mother, the Empress Dowager, who took great interest in hearing the accounts of my tour round the world,

---

[1] His own wife's sudden death (see p. 175).

the lives and habits of the European Sovereigns, and especially of the Queen-Empress Victoria.

"It is always gratifying to remember the kind reception afforded to me by your husband and your good self in Hawarden Castle, where we spent together the pleasant afternoons.

"May I pray for the longevity of the most distinguished living scholar and statesman your husband and your good self to enjoy the surroundings of your children and grandchildren.—I remain, yours very sincerely,

"LI HUNG CHANG."

FROM FREDERIC HARRISON

"38 WESTBOURNE TERRACE,
"*January* 6, 1897.

"DEAR MRS. GLADSTONE,—May I be suffered to join with all your many friends and millions and millions of Englishmen in wishing you and your husband all blessings in the year that we are entering?

"It will always be one of the great memories of my life that I have known and conversed with one who will live so long in the history of our country.

"I rejoice to hear from Mr. J. Morley and Lord Rendel the best news of the health of you both."

On May 19, 1898, Mr. Gladstone's illness came to a peaceful end. At 5 a.m. on Ascension Day he passed away.

From Queen Alexandra

"Sandringham, Norfolk,
"Whitsunday, May 29, 1898.

"Dearest Mrs. Gladstone,—I waited until *now*, when your beloved husband has been laid in his last resting-place, before daring to intrude on the sacredness of your sorrow, which I fear surpasses all that words can express. My telegram will, however, have told you how my thoughts and prayers have been constantly with and for you ever since the terrible news of his fatal illness first reached me. We are thankful to think that, after all his sufferings, his last few days were peaceful and painless, and that his longing and wish to go to his 'heavenly home' were granted him on the very day of Our Saviour's Ascension. It must be of some consolation to you also to feel how the whole nation mourns with you and yours the loss of that great and good man, whose name will go down in letters of gold to posterity as one of the most beautiful, upright, and disinterested characters that has ever adorned the pages of history. We all individually grieve the loss of a great personal friend from whom we have received innumerable kindnesses which we shall never forget. How my whole heart went out to you during Saturday's terrible ordeal, when I saw you kneeling by the side of the dear remains of him whom you loved best on earth—'the People's William,' and your all.

"I do hope your health has not suffered, and that the cross our dear Lord has laid upon you is not more than you can bear, and that for your dear children's sake you will take the greatest care of yourself. I was so deeply touched by your kind lines when you thought there was a ray of hope left, and you may be sure our visit to you and your beloved husband only one little year ago, in your own beautiful home at Hawarden, will ever remain as one of our most precious and valued memories.

" With deepest sympathy with you and your children.—Yours very affectionately,

"ALEXANDRA."

FROM SIR WILLIAM RICHMOND

"BEAVOR LODGE, HAMMERSMITH,
"*October* 29, 1898.

"MY DEAR MRS. GLADSTONE,—I return you my most affectionate thanks for the most precious and valuable memento which you have been so gracious as to give me.

"I assure you that I regard your kindness

with gratitude. It happens that the Poems of Michael Angelo have been for many years the object of my constant study; most of them I have translated, and I remember talking over their many beauties with Mr. Gladstone upon the occasion of my last walk with him a very few years ago. Now, you have given me *his* copy of those immortal works. Dear Mrs. Gladstone, please permit me to subscribe myself, your grateful and affectionate old friend, W. B. RICHMOND.

"I am most keen about the National Memorial, and desirous that the form it takes from an artistic point shall be worthy, beautiful, and dignified."

FROM SIR WILLIAM HARCOURT

"MALWOOD, LYNDHURST,
"*November* 25, '98.

"MY DEAR MRS. GLADSTONE,—I have received through your Harry a most precious gift of a book which belonged to Mr. Gladstone, as a memorial of one whom I do greatly love and honour, not more in his public greatness than in that singular personal kindness which he has ever bestowed on me and mine.

"The Herodotus is full of the marks of his reading, so varied and yet so exact, and brings back to me at every page his likeness as I knew him.

"I watch daily in my garden the growth of the walnut he planted here ten years ago, and the young ash tree, which will be historical monuments.

"The book will be a precious heirloom which will be treasured by my children's children, who will be proud to know that I served under such a commander."

Mr. and Mrs. Gladstone had spent the winter of 1866-67 in Rome, and Sir William Richmond, then a young and rising artist, was one of the party.

FROM SIR WILLIAM RICHMOND

"*January* 1, 1899.

"MY DEAR MRS. GLADSTONE,—You shall have the picture[1] very soon.

"I grieve for you, dear lady. This time of year brings back very sweet memories to me of Rome in '67. *How* kind you all were to me, and what a thing it was for a young fellow to be allowed to be the companion of your great and noble husband. My love to all of you.—Yours affectionately,

"W. B. RICHMOND."

[1] The drawing taken the day after his death by Sir William Richmond of Mr. Gladstone.

From Mrs. Benson

"5 Barton Street, Westminster,
"*Ascension Day*, 1899.

"Dearest Mrs. Gladstone,—I could not tell you how often and how deeply you have been in my heart all these months, and so specially on Ascension Day, and now.

"The power of anniversaries comes to some people much more fully than to others, and I can't help feeling that with you (as with me) it is scarcely possible for an anniversary to be fuller of the one thought and the one love, than all the other days. Oh, it must be so. What have *anniversaries* to do with it when it is the life of one's life ? Perhaps the feeling in the air and the look of everything in the trees and the flowers have a certain keenness, and perhaps they may help in this way—in bringing back the fulness of the glory of his departure and of the first days. For how my heart has ached for you during these months! I have trodden the same weary road, and know to the full what one could scarcely realise beforehand, the awful emptiness—the stagnation, as it seems, of everything; and for a time one's life has the old impetus in it, and then it ceases, and still the days and hours have to be lived through.

"And, dear friend, how I think of you to-day! For to-day you look off from the present to the glorious past, and to the wonderful future—and the reality lies there—for I suppose it is in a way one's own impatience which makes any empty present seem intolerable; it is really one with the fullest of one's life, and with the eternal crown of it all. Oh, forgive me for such weak words. My whole heart goes out to you, for I seem to know so well what there is to bear; but there are given such wonderful glimpses into the strength and consolations of God even when times are driest that I hope in my soul you all live in these—and to-day all the perfect part must be yours so specially. I often wonder so what 'a year' means in the eternal expression—glory and joy and growth—anyhow we shall know, and that soon. May I send my deepest and most reverent love to you, and much too to Mary, and to Lady Frederick, and remain, your loving and grateful MARY BENSON."

FROM LORD MORLEY

"57 ELM PARK GARDENS,
"SOUTH KENSINGTON, *May* 18, 1899.

"MY DEAR MRS. GLADSTONE,—When you receive this, we shall all be thinking of the same mournful thing. The year has gone quickly enough, but hardly a day has passed without that great loss being borne into my mind and heart. We all knew that it would leave our lives emptier; but how terrible the emptiness would often be we could not know. I do not want to write you a letter; but only to assure you of my sincere affection, and of my unalterable attachment to his memory.— Always yours, JOHN MORLEY."

CHAPTER VI

CHARACTERISTICS

WILLIAM and Catherine Gladstone were indeed a striking pair. She carried herself regally, though her movements were swift and light. Her eyes were of a deep sapphire blue, set well apart, long in shape, and with a world of meaning — eyes that danced with mischief or melted with tenderness — caressing eyes, capable of infinite love, infinite merriment. There is but one picture that has her eyes. It is one of Romney's most beautiful portraits of Lady Hamilton. So strong is the resemblance — the long laughing eyes, the dark curling hair — that at Tabley, in the famous picture gallery where it hangs, it used always to be called "Mrs. Gladstone."

She had an abundance of thick brown hair that waved softly upon her forehead. In figure she was tall and slender, and her movements were full of dignity and charm. Her husband used to say that, as he stood near the dais at a Drawing-room or Court, no one approached the Queen with so fine a carriage, or curtseyed with so much grace. And this was in spite of great rapidity, and even carelessness and indifference as to personal attire or adornment. She was clothed as by magic. She never shopped unless it was to buy for others. All she wore was made at home.[1] She spared but the merest fragment of her time to matters of dress or ornament. But she responded in a marked degree to any beauty of material, or form or colour; to a rare piece of old lace, to a jewel or a flower. On some women real jewels look sham, on others sham jewels look real. Jewels looked their best and most brilliant on her; so did flowers. She always wore a flower—a rose for choice. The first time she ever wore the blue velvet, afterwards an almost historic gown, she happened in the House of Commons to meet Lord Hartington :' " The first bit of blue sky I have seen to-day." This anecdote she related with much relish to Lady Edward Cavendish, his sister-in-law, Lord Hartington being uncommonly chary with his compliments.

She had a rare sympathy and understanding. As an illustration of the tact that comes from them: Soon after the Phœnix Park murders, a certain lady was continually alluding to Lord Frederick's wife as "Lady Cavendish."

[1] In her day, ladies' maids were skilled dressmakers.

"She likes to be called Lady Frederick Cavendish," said Mrs. Gladstone, "because, you see, she does so love his name." Indeed, she had a unique capacity for putting herself into other people's places, seeing with their eyes, feeling with their emotions, suffering or rejoicing with them. At evening parties and balls all her pity would go out to the tired attendants in the cloak-room, the footmen and link-boys outside, the poor little patient crowd on the pavement, waiting for a chance glimpse of jewels or fine clothes, a gleam of light, or a strain of far-off music—content with the fragments of a feast they would never share.

She was a great person for sharing. Mr. Gladstone used to smile as he declared that she was born without the sense of property. It amused him to call her a pickpocket. "You forgot to tell me," he once wrote, "for what cause you picked so-and-so's pocket?" He used to chaff her mercilessly on her mistakes; occasionally some unlucky mishap as to inviting the wrong person, or failing to send a carriage to meet a guest. Hawarden had the misfortune to possess half a dozen stations, which contributed not a little to these disasters. But once at Penmaenmawr, when a missing purse was actually found in her own pocket, after she had indignantly denied it, it is easy to imagine her

MRS. GLADSTONE
1863
A photograph taken for the Prince of Wales' Wedding Album

utter discomfiture, and the delight of the onlookers. She had entered a post office to buy stamps; a labouring man made way for her, leaving his purse on the counter. Her business accomplished, she mechanically swept his purse into her own pocket. Her onslaughts on the purses and possessions of her relations and friends in the cause of charity were a constant amusement and alarm to them all. She was really a Communist at heart; she could never enjoy anything by herself; it must be shared by the few or the many — the whole world if possible. She never had so many claims that she would not undertake a fresh one; she never had so many Homes depending on her that she was not ready for a new venture. She spent almost nothing on herself; she was generally overdrawn. She would give, if need be, anything off her own person. Nobody was so ragged, so friendless, so wretched, that she would not succour or save.

Apropos of her way of putting herself into the circumstances of other people, Lord Ribblesdale gives me an amusing instance. It was at Windsor, somewhere between 1880 and 1885.

" We were at luncheon," he writes—" that is, the background of the clatter and play of knife and fork, was daylight. . . . Some notable burglar, after a long series of inglorious, daring, and successful robberies (perhaps Peace ?), had been 'bagged.' And the papers were full of the actual and psychological eccentricities of his character and career. Mr. Gladstone had something to say on both, and it was then that your mother, dismissing summarily the metaphysical aspect of the affair, broke in. She said she always sympathised with those who, like Peace, after a full and exciting life, find themselves condemned to the tedium and dullness of prison ('dull and dullness' were her defining words). Mrs. G. said this quite naturally and in much the same way as if she was commenting on a picnic being spoilt by rain.

"Mr. G., who was still in the full swing of his metaphysical investigations, at first looked at her with something like indignation—the expression of his eyes darkened and concentrated on, as it were, a new foeman.

"He then was amused—and his eyes, too—nor do I ever recollect having seen him laugh so unrestrainedly and playfully—'the heart's laugh,' as it were. The Queen was there and laughed too.

"Actual words I can't give—only the general setting and its impression on me."

How vivid is this picture!—the triumph in the capture of so redoubtable a miscreant, the discussion on his unique personality. " But oh how dull he will be—conceive the utter dullness of a prison ! " One can hear her very words—Mr. Gladstone's gravity broken down as he realised her attitude—his laughter —and the amusement of the Queen !

One day, going to her Convalescent Home at Woodford, she was quickly so absorbed in the pitiful tale of a fellow-traveller, quite unknown to her, that she forgot to alight at her own station, and had to borrow from the poor lady to enable her to get back to her destination. That night at a dinner-party she collected sixty or seventy pounds, and having asked the lady to visit her next day, was able to get her passage to Australia, so saving her a separation from her husband. (The said husband was highly sceptical of his wife's story. " Well, you *have* been taken in. The idea of Mrs. Gladstone travelling third class, and without any money ! I shall come with you and wait outside the house.")

Many and many instances crowd in upon the memory, but this anecdote will suffice to show her abounding sympathy, and the consummate ease with which she leapt over difficulties that would have checkmated any- one else. " For I was an hungered, and ye gave Me meat; I was thirsty, and ye gave Me drink; I was a stranger, and ye took Me in; I was sick and ye visited Me; I was in prison, and ye came unto Me." Could any words more fitly describe her?

She would get more into one crowded hour than most people would into a day. She would be in the East End of London at one moment and at the House of Commons the next—no motor bus, or car, or taxi in those days. On foot, by underground, cab, or carriage, she performed these weary journeys. Often dead tired, and with a final climb of eighty-six steps to the Ladies' Gallery (no lift in those days), yet somehow or other, alive or dead, she usually contrived to be in her corner when her husband was going to speak.

Unpunctual by nature, she never kept him waiting, realising the value of the few moments more or less. Ever at his side on all important or anxious occasions, she contrived to keep the manifold activities and businesses of her own life subordinate to his. A carriage at a moment's notice, her own or anybody else's, always available for his needs; meals ready at any and every minute that he might escape from the House (it made heavier demands on its Members in those days). Astute at warding off bores or toadies, or tiresome or tiring people, she saw through them quickly; she would put in her word or sign of warning long before his guileless nature had detected anything below the surface. He could always be deceived, for, like Lord Melbourne, "he had a habit of believing people," and not only believing people but believing *in* people. He judged others by his own standards, and, as was once said of him by a famous contemporary historian, "he did not always make bull's-eyes." She was far more acute in her judgment of character. She would have made a good general. She husbanded her resources, she never wasted powder, and she knew how to dispose of her materials to the best advantage. She was a strategist of the first order, and was a woman of infinite courage and resource. She was impatient of routine, of control; she loved adventure; she rose to the call, whatever it might be; she lived in every fibre of her being. She drank eagerly of all that life had to offer. "Nothing venture, nothing have." She might have been the author of that proverb.

"You felt her splendid intuition, her swift motions, the magic of her elusive phrases, her rapid courage, her never-failing fund of sympathy, her radiance, her gaiety of heart, her tenderness of response."[1]

No matter where she was or where she went,

[1] Rev. H. S. Holland.

nothing could remain dull or stupid. "Her presence brought an atmosphere," said Mr. George Russell, "a climate with it, all brightness, freshness, like sunshine and sea air."

She somehow always seemed to raise the temperature of a room, morally and physically, whether full of bored, stodgy grown-ups or shy, self-conscious boys and girls, or sick people in a hospital ward. By the magic touch of her personality she woke them up, made them laugh or sing or dance. She set things going; she made things happen; she got things done. While her love and pity were all-enfolding, her gaiety, the airy grace of her movements were all infectious. Katharine Lyttelton remembers, in her young days, the sense of comfort and capacity she gave:

"Children felt, especially in times of anxiety or distress, that somebody had arrived who was going to help, to solve difficulties, to light up the road, and, incidentally, to make fun for all concerned. She radiated tenderness."

Katharine's sister, Lady Lovelace, continues:

"At such dark times, dear Aunty Pussy would come as a fresh breeze in summer, bringing life and courage to old and young. I can hear now the gay voice at the door, before she had turned the handle, 'Well, darlings!' and I see her come in with arms outstretched, into which we all tumbled. And she would sit among us and laugh and joke and tell us stories, all in her queer, humorous, family slang, which has been immortalised by her brother-in-law.[1] And all the time we could see the tears in her beautiful eyes, and, young as we were, we knew that it was because she felt to her heart's core that she was making us merry.

"Many years ago, in our childhood, one of her daughters and two Lyttelton boys were shut up in a St. Leonards lodging-house on the Marine Parade. She used to come each morning and, regardless of onlookers, dance in front of our windows. I can see her now as we watched, fascinated, every movement full of gaiety and grace."

As to her genius in the sick-room one of her nieces[2] writes:

"Few people have possessed a finer instinct in illness than Aunty Pussy, added to a quite heroic unselfishness in devoting herself in a sick-room where she knew she was really wanted, or where her deep mother's love for one of her belongings brought her to the bedside.

So it was in May's long, pathetic illness in

---

[1] Lord Lyttelton's *Glynnese Glossary*.
[2] Lavinia Lyttelton (Mrs. E. S. Talbot).

January 1875. Directly she realised the nature of the illness, she pushed aside family, social, political engagements, and what was the greatest sacrifice of all—leaving her husband at one of the most anxious moments of his political life.

"I shall never forget what she was to us at Hagley during the nine weeks of May's[1] almost hopeless illness. The mere fact of her presence in the room meant so much, with her inspiring ways and tone of voice. She had, moreover, an unusual instinct, quick and unerring in detecting symptoms and changes, whether bad or good, and we relied on her judgment and accurate recognition of the true state of things. She was full of resourcefulness in little things, often going beyond the doctors, and her tender, patient watchfulness never failed.

"She encouraged and inspired the nurses, fascinated and impressed the doctors—she supplemented them all. I remember seeing her on the bed for hours, in a tiring, strained attitude, helping to keep an ice-bag exactly in the right position on the head of the patient. And she was, what is perhaps rarer, wise and careful in garnering up her own strength as well as that of those sharing the watching, and no one knew better how to have a real rest.

[1] Mary Lyttelton, third daughter of Lord Lyttelton.

"Then her fun—never very far off—seeing the humorous side of things even in deepest anxiety, giving such racy accounts of her experiences, and such true ones, too, both in talk and in writing.

"And when the end drew near, and we knew our darling May was not to stay with us, there shone out from her what was indeed present all through—her beautiful submission and strong faith and certainty that we were in the hands of a loving Father; while sharing it so deeply, she helped us to face the overwhelming grief of that young death by her tender love and brave, Christian bearing."

One of her grandsons,[1] as he looks back upon his childhood, makes special mention of Mrs. Gladstone's fertility of ideas in dealing with children — how she ministered to his self-respect, his belief in his own capacities. At the age of three and a half he was imprisoned at the Castle by scarlet fever, and when sent to convalesce at Rhyl, instead of equipping him with the indispensable bucket and spade, she engaged him to sweep up the leaves in the Castle garden at sixpence a day. Bursting with pride—"I bought my own appliances for castle-building out of my own money which I had earned." Again, ten

[1] W. G. Wickham.

years later, once more she played fairy godmother.

Instead of getting tickets for the play in the normal manner, she gave the boy a guinea, telling him he was to treat his mother to the play. Oh, the honour and glory of that guinea!

"As I had only been about three times before to a theatre, and had never previously been in a position to treat anyone to anything, my pride in that brief moment in the booking office was unforgettable.

"I give these two episodes because they have always seemed to me so typical of her. It was not merely that she seemed to live in one continuous round of thinking of small or large kindnesses to all about her, but that she appeared to be endowed with such a peculiar gift, amounting to genius, for devising uncommon ways of conferring these, as to impress them on grateful memories in a way that no one else could have done."

A characteristic anecdote will not come amiss illustrative of her resourcefulness, her husband's unsuspiciousness. It was one winter in the 'eighties, at a time when Irish troubles and threatening letters obliged the Home Office to appoint detectives to shadow Mr. Gladstone even at Hawarden. He and Mrs.

Gladstone and their daughter Helen were to dine and sleep at Soughton Hall,[1] a neighbouring country house. An hour or so before the hour fixed for starting, word came from the stables that the coachman had injured his hand too badly for him to drive. No one else could be trusted to drive the rather fresh pair of horses. The only fly in the village had been requisitioned by the detectives. What was to be done? Mr. Gladstone was the last person to be told. Lord and Lady Aberdeen were staying at the Castle, and quickly Mrs. Gladstone and Lord Aberdeen cut the Gordian knot. The latter would drive. It was dark, so Mr. W. H. Gladstone would play the part of footman, sit on the box, show him the way, and return with him to Hawarden. Mr. Gladstone, in the innocence of his heart, hunted for his guest to bid him good-bye. Lady Aberdeen played the game, joined in the hunt, and finally made his excuses, and took the farewell message. They drove off, and the following day the favourite little foreign maid, who was inside the carriage with Mr. and Mrs. Gladstone and their daughter, wrote the following account of it to Lady Aberdeen:

"Not many yards beyond the Castle gate, somehow the question arose about carriage

[1] The home of Rt. Hon. Lord Justice Sir J. Eldon Bankes.

coming back. 'But the carriage puts up at Soughton?' 'No, dear, I thought it best for you to return to-morrow in the Victoria.' 'How is that?—a strange thing to change plans.' 'Oh, mama, you'd better tell father the truth.' 'Very well, now we're safe on the way—we have had the most bothering affair.' [Mrs. Gladstone then explains to him the whole contretemps, as interpreted by the maid in the most racy language.] 'But where is Zadock?' 'Oh, don't bother yourself, father; it will be all right.' Mr. Gladstone having gradually looked at the thing with merry eyes, burst out laughing, and a most joyous glee took place. The carriage was jugging along slow but sure, lodge past, a stray gate arrived, and suddenly a figure flew past carriage window, and Mr. Gladstone called out, 'Why, there is Zadock opening the gate' [Mr. Gladstone's valet]. 'Most extraordinary proceedings; we must be in fairyland.' Another glee took place, the door of House was reached, Mr. W. H. Gladstone, footmanlike, jumped down from box and put the luggage inside front door. Alas, the delightful Wonderland came to an end. Had I known I was to write this I would have had pencil and paper in carriage. —Your Ladyship's humble,

"AUGUSTE SCHLÜTER."

The letter in full, cleverly gives the characteristics of the three speakers in the carriage, so that each is unmistakable, though the writer gives no names.

Early in their married life her husband gave Mrs. Gladstone the choice between knowing all or nothing. It will easily be guessed that she made the choice which gave her most share in his life. He told her everything. Lord Harcourt, the Lou-lou of those days, who knew her very intimately, makes the following comment in a letter: "Her discretion as to public secrets, *of which she knew all*, was really extraordinary; she was willing, if necessary, to allow herself in conversation to appear almost a fool, in order to conceal the fact of her knowledge." A good judge remarked that there was an unmistakable element of greatness in her character, which justified the name by which she was known in intimate circles — the "*grande dame*."

Her energy, her spirit were almost superhuman, but she was capable of absolute repose. She would lie down quietly upon the sofa, as if she had not a duty or a care in the world, and fall into profound sleep for a few minutes. There was a singular beauty and charm in her look and pose as she lay sleeping—the wavy hair, the slightly parted lips, the look of utter peace—and she would wake up as a new being, absolutely rested and refreshed.

If within the bounds of possibility, she never deviated from this rule of lying down to rest before dinner. In the multifarious energies of her life she found this habit a really marvellous pick-me-up. Sometimes for an hour's sleep, often for ten or five minutes only. How she could endure the torture of the sudden enforced awakening—sometimes at the last gasp of fatigue—is only to be explained by the self-control she had acquired in all matters that touched her husband, by the rigidity of her rule never to keep him waiting even for a moment. From the deepest, dreamless sleep up she would leap, and in an incredibly short time she would appear, like Cinderella at the touch of the fairy wand, in her evening attire—wreathed, shod, gloved, jewelled, to delight the eyes of the long-suffering foreign maid [1] and of any who chanced to see her.

She had no mind or patience for intricate questions, for the details of history, or science or theology. These she disposed of as " red tape."

" She contrived," writes Lady Lovelace, " to combine the keenest interest and quick apprehension of all that concerned her hus-

---

[1] "We had no time," she said. "Mrs. Gladstone just *yumped* into her clothes."

band's career, with the most unashamed boredom with politics in general. If her respect for his opinions bordered on veneration, she could not always restrain an impish desire to interrupt the expression of them. At the dinner-table there was sure to be some one who would do his best to draw out the greatest statesman of the day upon some serious subject, and when we were all rather drooping under the consideration of how to compensate the Irish Clergy, or how to deal electorally with the Compound Householder, it was to her that we looked for relief. And sure enough sooner or later, with a rapid wink at the youngest of us, she would dart into some interstice of the conversation with a comic remark, or bit of refreshing gossip, which brought an instant change of atmosphere."

There were some who were impatient of these interruptions, however comic and clever, but her husband was always understanding and sympathetic, looking at her with a whimsical look in his eyes—what she called in one of her letters "that happy, wicked look." And if it *really* mattered, she had an instinct, an intuition amounting to genius—a mind that leaped over every complication and somehow or other, by hook or by crook, landed on the right spot, and said and did and looked the right thing.

In *A Visit to Hawarden*,[1] Lady Ribblesdale aptly hits her off.

"Mrs. Gladstone was sitting with us round the tea-table, enjoying, not adding to, the talk. She listened in her own fugitive, happy way; whatever the topic, she seemed to master all she needed with three seconds' airy inattention. Her quick sympathy enabled her to pick up anything she fancied, and if her understanding was instinctive rather than intellectual, it was seldom at fault."

And Laura Lyttelton, at Hawarden in 1885, writes to her sister-in-law:

" . . . and my chiefest among ten thousand was Auntie Pussy. I did love her so." (Drawing of a puss.)

"People say there is nothing so warm as a bed in the snow. If that's true, then Auntie Pussy is the snow bed. She is quite as white in that blessed old soul—*young* soul, I mean—of hers, quite as sparkling as snow in the sun, quite as deep and soft and quite as warm—and warmer. . . ."

She had the unusual gift of acting on the spur of the minute. With accurate judgment she saw by intuition the psychological moment;

[1] *Nineteenth Century Review.*

she would leap into the arena while others were hesitating on the brink, waiting for a sign, asking themselves what could be done, like Browning's pair in "Dis aliter visum." Everybody's business is nobody's business. Sir Charles Ryan told me of his lifelong gratitude to her for coming to the rescue at the most embarrassing moment of his life. He was being married to Miss Shaw Lefevre in July 1862, at St. Martin's-in-the-Fields, in the presence of the usual London crowd. When the time came for him to place the ring on the finger of the bride, it refused to go on— the ring was too small. An awkward pause ensued—paralysis on the part of the guests— when Mrs. Gladstone was seen rapidly making her way through the crowd, and as she reached the neighbourhood of the bridal pair, drawing her own wedding-ring off her own finger, she put it in the hand of Sir Charles. He slipped it on, it fitted, and the situation was retrieved. Yet she was always almost superstitious about her wedding-ring and could never bear to be without it.

Lord Rosebery reminds me of another incident during the first Midlothian Campaign, which greatly amused and delighted him. One afternoon we drove from Dalmeny to a neighbouring town for an election meeting, and called on the chief magnate of the place. The meeting was timed for three o'clock; we had just had luncheon, and were somewhat dismayed at finding five o'clock tea ready for us at half-past two. It was suggested we should return after the meeting and partake of this hospitality. What was Mrs. Gladstone's horror, after the meeting was over and we went back to the house, to find that the tea had been stewing on the hob during the intervening hours—the very same tea that was offered at two-thirty! The first cup was almost like treacle when it was handed to her husband. But even then her resource did not fail her. No conjurer could have been more nimble. She sauntered towards her husband, deftly took the cup and, concealing it beneath her mantle, she suddenly betrayed a longing to behold the view. Quietly and swiftly she moved towards the window, and, unseen by the company, she contrived to pour the offending liquid into the garden below.

Here is one more instance: Mr. and Mrs. Gladstone had flitted up to London during the Recess, and were staying in Harley Street for a day or two—there was practically no household, and they had arranged to go to luncheon with their next-door neighbour. They were on the point of starting when the bell rang and Lord Granville was shown in.

"Can you give me some luncheon?" he said. Mr. Gladstone was just about to explain that unfortunately there was no luncheon, and that they were going out for luncheon. What was his surprise when Mrs. Gladstone broke in before he could answer—"Oh yes, dear Lord Granville, too delighted to have you." Such was her husband's confidence in her powers of resource, that he veiled his astonishment and drew Lord Granville into the empty dining-room for his talk.

Like a scene in a play, presently the door opened; footmen entered with trays; the cloth was laid, the table dressed, the butler brought in wine, etc. Mrs. Gladstone had quietly slipped out of the house and brought back with her the whole contingent—hostess, servants, and food—from next door. Chuckling with delight, Mr. Gladstone seated himself at the head of the table, and turning to his hostess, now by a miracle changed into his guest: "May I have the pleasure of giving you some of this excellent pie? I have special reason for highly commending it," etc. etc.

The spontaneity and impulsiveness of her nature, of her movements, her actions, her words, while distinctly adding to the charm, sometimes resulted in laughable situations. Rash and impetuous as she was, it will easily be believed that occasionally she made a *faux pas*; but if by chance she did come to grief, no one was ever so quick at recovery, so alert at finding an escape, so nimble at turning the tables on her adversary.

A friend who met her at dinner in the 'nineties relates the following incident. It aptly illustrates her knack of carelessly appropriating to herself the vantage-ground, when quite unmistakably belonging to her adversary. She was seated next to Mr. Jacob Bright, and looked frankly bored. Presently she broke the silence in a desperate sort of way:

" And how is your brother ? "

" My brother, John Bright, is no more."

Mrs. Gladstone.—" Oh, I know that—of course I did not mean him. I meant your other brother."

Jacob Bright.—" But I never had any other brother, Mrs. Gladstone."

Mrs. Gladstone.—" Yes, yes, I knew him quite well; fatter than you—he sat for Stoke and resigned his seat on account of ill-health."

Jacob Bright (cheering up and pleased at being mistaken for his brother's son).—" Oh, that is not my brother—I only wish I was not too old to claim a brother so young. The one you mean is my nephew, William Leatham Bright, my brother John's son."

Mrs. Gladstone (smiling complacently and compassionately).—" Ah ! I see you make the same mistake I sometimes do and confuse the generations."

(Total discomfiture of Jacob Bright, who saw that, somehow or other, the victory did not lie with him. She was over eighty at the time, but had not lost the elasticity of her mind.)

Explanations, wordiness, "trolls,"[1] bored and bothered her. She wanted to get without delay to the point; if possible to sum up in one pregnant word or phrase, something like a flash of lightning. Always she preferred short-cuts, leaving things to the imagination. The keynote of the *Glynnese Glossary* (for many of whose expressions she surely must have been responsible) is ellipsis, short-cuts—" *Than which* "—see Lord Lyttelton's admirable example and explanation. "I have been half an hour teaching Albert to write—*than which*."

"It is evident," says Lord Lyttelton, " that to assimilate this sentence to any recognised form of expression, nothing less than some enormous ellipse is required—' than which nothing more bothering or tedious can possibly be imagined.' It is spoken in a tone of despairing good-humour, and with a sort of combined smile, sigh, and shake of the head."

This characteristic often led her to join up or " telescope " proverbs or phrases : " The will has been declared vull," she said. " Do

[1] Glynnese for prosiness.

you mean null and void?" asked her matter-of-fact interlocutor. "No, dear, I always say *vull*." He "put up his nose" (turned up his nose and put up his back), "riding a vicycle" (bicycle and vehicle). "The cat will be in the fire" (letting the cat out of the bag does put the fat in the fire). These were not the ordinary Malapropisms of Sheridan. They were her very own Bonapropisms, significant of ideas, impressions she wished rapidly and acutely to convey. With her amazing handiness at making good shots, at "twigging" on only fragmentary data (which she called "seeing with an eye"), it is not odd that she was often apt to credit others with her own, quick intuitions, greatly to their discomfiture and to her own amazement, should they not rise to the occasion.

"Thus she would severely complain if certain plans or directions were not carried out, for the simple reason that she had omitted to supply the necessary details. On such occasions an aggrieved niece [1] would dub her 'Nebuchadnezzar,' because he expected his magicians, on pain of death, not only to interpret his dream but to tell him the dream he had dreamed."

But it is very hard, no doubt, to give a true picture of her humour, so curious a blending

[1] Lady F. Cavendish.

was she of the casual and the concentrated. She had a heavenly sense of fun, but its manner of expression was all her own. There was nothing on earth to compare to the twinkle in her eye. And she was really witty in her own way, though only half-consciously so; " hers was the incarnation of mother-wit, not only in conversation but in the conduct of life generally—wit in the widest sense, including gravity and wisdom." She was ever a source of affectionate amusement to those who knew her well. One of those blessed beings you laughed with, at and for, and whichever it was she and you enjoyed it.

Coming out from family prayers one morning, " Mumble major," so she summed up the reading of our host. Of a good-hearted, bustling lady she would say, " In she walked with her *here I am* hat." Asked to describe a lady's dress (of rather questionable reputation), after picturing the general effect, she paused: " As to the body—well—I can only describe it as a *look at me* body." On another occasion she was speaking about the unloverlike relations of a newly engaged couple: " To be sure," she said, " they did sit side by side upon the couch; but they looked just like a coachman and footman on the box, so stiff and upright, *you could always see the light between.*"

Daily she would be off on some errand of personal service, some act of love or sympathy; a smile, a sigh, a tear. Never did she seem to lose sight of the needs of others. She would scarcely enjoy a mouthful of food without remembering some one—perhaps in the village, or Home of Rest, or Orphanage—less well supplied with worldly goods. "Cut off a wing," she would say to the long-suffering butler, "and let it go hot to Miss R. *at once.*" On the mantelpiece in the hall was usually to be seen some tit-bit she had purloined from the luncheon-table on the chance of somebody going up to the village. "Never go to bed at night," she said to her children, "without the feeling you have done some little act of kindness or selflessness."

Nowadays she might have belonged to the P.B.S.,[1] so few words did she waste. Her time also she never wasted. Up to her eighty-fifth year, she did not walk upstairs, she ran.

But she could hardly be called an ideal Prime Minister's wife, any more than he could be chosen as the type of an ideal Prime Minister. His conscientiousness was often tiresome to and misunderstood by his colleagues; both of them were too much absorbed in their several "works" to fulfil small social duties with much success; they were neither of them gifted with

[1] Preservation of Breath Society.

MRS. GLADSTONE AT HAWARDEN
1893

From a portrait by J. McLure Hamilton

the royal eye, and—fatal fault—frequently mistook one person for another. She was careless and neglectful as to returning calls. Lord Acton always regretted that there was so little system as to small civilities in society, or as he called it, "greasing the wheels"—*i.e.* dropping hundreds of cards, keeping immaculate lists of callers, of politicians carefully differentiated, into groups, to be coaxed, flattered, noticed, looked after; wandering sheep to be led back to the Liberal fold. There was, indeed, but little of this necessary work. He was up to his eyes in graver issues of State, and she was absorbed in schemes chiefly humanitarian.

As we look back upon the fruitful years of this long and crowded life, we seem to recognise how the chief characteristics of the child, as seen in Chapter I., determination of purpose and "enthusiasm of humanity," have been throughout its mainspring. The dauntless will enabled her to surmount all difficulties, the loving heart to guide the will in the paths of righteousness.

Infallible she was not; she had her naughtinesses; she was wayward; she was wilful; she made her mistakes; they were *les défauts de ses qualités*. But she had a heart of gold; the eternal child was in her, and of such is the Kingdom of Heaven.

It would be vain to attempt anything really approaching to a Life of Mrs. Gladstone under several volumes. Any reader who possibly may be kindled into a longing to know more of her fourscore years and eight must have recourse to the Biography[1] of her husband. There can be in existence few books more elevating to the mind, more kindling to the spirit, more profoundly interesting both historically and personally. In these volumes only can be found the full record of her outer life—of the mighty triumphs, of the overwhelming anxieties, the hours of suspense, the trials and disappointments that she shared with him. But whether in defeat or whether in victory, in sorrow or in joy, they were one in mind and soul.

> "If any two creatures grew into one,
> They would do more than the world has done.
> Though each apart were never so weak,
> Ye vainly through the world should seek
> For the knowledge and the might
> Which in such union grew their right." [2]

The duration of their married life was nearly threescore years and ten, throughout which time their lives were closely interwoven; everything that concerned him touched the very roots of her being. They acted and reacted on one another, and without the thrill

---

[1] *Life of W. E. Gladstone*, by Lord Morley.
[2] *The Flight of the Duchess*, by Browning.

and profound interest of his life, hers would have been an absolutely different matter.

Without her, it is likely that he would still have made an indelible mark on history, but much of the lighter side, the charm, the fun, would have been lost. Without him, her life would have lacked public importance and interest, but in whatever circumstances or conditions she had been born, she would have stirred the waters; she would have made things hum; nothing approaching dullness or stagnation could have existed in her presence.

No one knew him better in later life than Lord Morley, no one can have studied more deeply every phase of his career and character. Mrs. Gladstone, in a conversation with him in 1891, spoke of her husband's two opposing sides—the one impetuous, impatient, irrestrainable; the other all self-control, able to dismiss everything but the great central aim, to put aside all that was weakening or disturbing—that he had achieved this complete mastery of self, and had succeeded in the dire struggle ever since he was three- or four-and-twenty. This conquest he had won first by the natural grit of his character; second by ceaseless wrestling in prayer—prayer that had been abundantly answered.

"If he sometimes recalls a fiery hero of the 'Iliad,'" says Lord Morley, "at other times, he is the grave and studious Benedictine, but whether in quietude or movement, always a man inspired with a purpose. He was an idealist, yet ever applying ideals to their purposes in act."

Mrs. Gladstone, perhaps not unnaturally, regarded her husband's speaking as absolutely unequalled, above that of every orator living or dead. How far did she exaggerate this pre-eminence ? Mr. Balfour paid it a notable tribute in the House of Commons, May 19, 1898 ; Lord Morley's more analytic description is a masterpiece, but Lord Acton surely sums it up best of all :

" He alone possessed all the qualities of the orator. Whether he prepared an oration or hurled a reply, whether he addressed a British mob or the cream of Italian politicians, and would be still the same if he spoke in Latin to Convocation."

" Shall I be short and precise ? " Mr. Gladstone asked his chief before rising to reply in debate. " No," said Sir Robert Peel, " be long and diffuse. It is all-important in the House of Commons to state your case in many different ways."

Yet no one sympathised more truly with those who listened to him : " I had to make an oration to which they listened with admirable patience."

The first time, as a child, he ever had to listen to a sermon (at St. George's, Liverpool), he remembered turning quickly to his mother: "Will he soon have done?"

It was seen, quite in early days, that he was a man of lion heart. Three men he used to recognise as possessing in a supreme degree the virtue of Parliamentary courage—Sir Robert Peel, Lord John Russell, and Mr. Disraeli.

"Toil was his natural element." He worked hard every day of the year, every hour of the day. Whatever he did, he did with all his might. Yet he often felt the longing for repose.

"The tumult of business," he wrote, "follows and whirls me day and night." And again, "A day restless as the sea."

And the following letter to Lord Lyttelton reveals the modesty and even self-distrust of his nature:

"It is my nature to lean not so much on the applause as upon the assent of others to a degree which perhaps I do not show, from that sense of weakness and utter inadequacy to my work which never ceases to attend me while I am engaged upon these subjects. . . . I wish you knew the state of total impotence to which I should be reduced if there were no echo to the accents of my own voice. I go through my labour, such as it is, not by a genuine elasticity of spirit, but by a plodding movement only just able to contend with inert force, and in the midst of a life which indeed has little claim to be called active, yet is broken this way and that into a thousand small details certainly unfavourable to calm and continuity of thought."

And to his wife in December 1841 he wrote of his craving for tranquillity—of his need of quiescence at home during the Parliamentary Session. He speaks of her presence and that of her sister Mary as alone never jarring or disturbing his "mental rest." But he adds, "There is no *man*, however near to me, with whom I am fit to live when hard worked."

With all his gravity of temperament, those who knew him best would never deny the gaiety of his heart. Sincerity and simplicity were the dominant notes of his character— both quite compatible with subtlety of intellect—and kindness was the habit of his mind. No loving enterprise of hers ever came amiss to him. He trusted to her intuition, and was ever ready to co-operate with her financially or otherwise. Were we all of us moved by the loving-kindness that characterised these two, there would be little more misery in the world.

There is no doubt he was formidable at times, especially when carried away by righteous indignation, but not one of his children or grandchildren was ever in awe of him, or indeed failed to treat him more or less as an equal. Stern in self-judgment, he was infinitely gentle to the weak, the erring, and the fallen.

It is by no means easy to place his sense of humour. It is denied to him by those who only experienced the intensity of his earnestness. Sir Charles Dilke says: " Mr. Gladstone was always of a playful mind, and whatever his absorption in the subject, would break off to discuss some amusing triviality."

This would hardly be a usual view of him. Mrs. Asquith was surprised to discover his great appreciation of Heine, having resolved that his sense of humour would not be sufficiently subtle. Of playfulness his speeches give a thousand proofs, and no one would deny his alacrity of mind. But there is no doubt Lord Morley is right when he says: " It was not always easy to be sure beforehand what sort of jest would hit or miss."

There can be no doubt that Mrs. Gladstone

stimulated his sense of humour, and that very often it saved the situation. He was quick in seeing the humour of a situation if not too deeply absorbed in its other aspects. Many an amusing poem or satire he dashed off on the spur of the moment, and one of his chiefest delights was to discover words for which it was difficult to find rhymes—*e.g.* his poem to Margot and his address to Parkins and Gotto. These would be found among his papers at St. Deiniol's.[1]

One anecdote may be recorded as illustrating the way Mrs. Gladstone had schooled her husband to jump with her:

"Oh, William, only think, so exciting. The Cook and the Captain are going to be married! (This was her morning's news from her Convalescent Home.) Apparently he took no notice; seemingly absorbed in his own thoughts, he absently stretched out his hand for a sheet of notepaper and began to write. "Oh, of course, you are too full of Homer and your old gods and goddesses to care—stupid of me!"

For a few minutes he went on writing, then handing her the paper—"There! that's all I can do, your information was so very scanty." And there was a poetic skit in three stanzas entitled:

[1] St. Deiniol's Library at Hawarden.

THE COOK AND THE CAPTAIN

"The Cook and the Captain determined one day,
When worthy Miss Simmons was out of the way,
On splicing together a life and a life,
The one as a husband the other as wife—
  Fol de rol, tol de rol, fol de rol la.

The Captain a subaltern officer made,
But the Cook! *she* was monarch of all she surveyed—
So how could they hit it the marrying day,
If she was to order and he to obey?
  Fol de rol, tol de rol, fol de rol la.

Miss Simmons came home and she shouted, 'Oh dear!
What riot is this? What the d——l is here?
If the Cook and the Captain will not be quiescent,
How can I expect it from each Convalescent?'
  Fol de rol, tol de rol, fol de rol la."

Mr. G. W. E. Russell, who visited Hawarden more than once, notices the genial, lighter side of their life as inexpressibly attractive. One of the unexpected incidents which most surprised and pleased him was their custom, in special moments of exhilaration, of standing with arms round each other on the hearth-rug, swaying as they sang:

"A ragamuffin husband and a rantipoling wife,
  We'll fiddle it and scrape it through the ups and downs of life."

She hardly ever had occasion to complain of his restlessness during sleepless nights. His iron self-control allowed him to keep rigidly quiet—he remembered the words of his "beloved physician."[1] "If you make up your mind, when you cannot sleep, to lie still,

---
[1] Sir Andrew Clark.

little will be lost of your rest." There are but three known occasions that he departed from this rule. In 1844, the two pairs of honeymooners were again at Fasque. *Ellen Middleton*[1] was just published. Mr. Gladstone was so engrossed by its absorbing interest that he read it all the night through; while the emotion broke his brother-in-law[2] into tears. In 1868, the question of Mr. Bright's inclusion in the Cabinet cost him his night's rest.

But on the night of May 6, 1882, the day that Lord Frederick Cavendish was murdered, he was unable to lie still. He and Mrs. Gladstone had been with their niece in Carlton House Terrace until the small hours of the morning of May 7. This tragedy touched them both to the quick; they loved their niece's husband with a parental love. No young man, with the possible exception of Mr. Balfour, was ever more dear to them. That night restlessness overmastered him. Finally he left his bed and composed the poem in twenty verses, which ends with these words:

> "And thou, O Mourner, lift thine head,
> And see this jewel of thy love
> With earthly soil no more bestead,
> And safe for ever stored above.
>
> He suffereth no more, nor dieth,
> Nor wandereth now in twilights dim.
> In light and rest and peace he lieth,
> The prayers of millions follow him."

---
[1] By Lady Georgiana Fullerton.   [2] Lord Lyttelton.

Diverse as they were in character and temperament, what was the secret of their abiding love for one another, their joy through a span of life nearly twenty years longer than that usually allotted to man?

They were moved by the same ardour to gather the very best, the richest out of life. To them life was not a thing to be idled and pleasured away; it was a sacred trust that implied true and laudable service to God and man. They lifted it to a new level. To them every additional child added a glory to their home. She revelled in the priceless blessing of his perfect trust, even while he might occasionally be bewildered by her daring exploits.

With them to pity was to act. "I don't think much of their pity, when it does not touch their pockets," so said an old woman as she left a parish meeting. But their emotions were never stirred in vain. One might reasonably think that the unavoidable daily grind of life is ample discipline in moulding and chastening the human character. But the highest development of self-restraint is seen at its best in those who gladly and voluntarily offer service, grappling perhaps daily with the first temptation that awaits them—the temptation to lie in bed. Mr. Gladstone once owned that the struggle never grew less, that custom did not ease the battle, that it was as hard to get daily out of bed for the uphill trudge to morning service after he was eighty as when he was half that age. The habit of self-mastery at normal times gives the victory at a crisis. And the crown of the conflict was witnessed by her courage and self-command during the winter and spring of 1898, and in him during his final illness, when the spirit rose triumphant over the flesh and in the greatest anguish of body enabled him to give thanks.[1]

To both of them religion was the master-key of life. Mr. Gladstone never thought of the Church but as the soul of the State. In every act the religious motive was predominant. In everything he thought, said, and did, he took for granted that right and wrong depended on the same principles in public as in private life. It has been truly said, " He lived and wrought in the sunlight."

While he laboured inside and outside the walls of Parliament to lighten the burdens of those least fitted to bear them, she used her gifts and graces in strengthening and sweetening and purifying the sad, the lonely, the sinful, the suffering, whether poor or rich, weak or powerful; with both hands she gave her love, her strength, her pity, her succour, to those who needed them.

[1] Oftenest in the words of Newman's hymn, " Praise to the Holiest."

It has been said of him, "He so lived and wrought that he kept the soul alive in England."[1] And if he kept the soul, she kept the heart alive. In truth, the secret lay in their devotion to Him, "Whose service is perfect freedom."

[1] For he divined "that laws should be adapted to those who have the heaviest stake in the country, those to whom misgovernment means, not mortified pride, or stinted luxury, but want and pain and degradation, and risk to their own lives and to their children's souls."—*Lord Acton's Letters.*

CHAPTER VII

GOOD WORKS

"She stretched out her hands to the poor, in her tongue was the law of kindness."

THIS chapter on Mrs. Gladstone's "good works" is mostly taken from an In Memoriam, written by one of whom it may be said, that though not of Catherine Gladstone's own flesh and blood, she loved and served her, perhaps more than any other, "to the uttermost and to the end."[1]

Mrs. Gladstone had the genius of Charity. She could, much more than was often known, elaborate a plan and set a work going on large, wise foundations.

With a houseful of children and grandchildren, of nephews and nieces, and a husband to whom she was utterly devoted, she might easily have produced the favourite plea of "no time," and it would have appeared a satisfactory one. But Mrs. Gladstone had a larger conception of duty and of love; with her

[1] Lucy, daughter of Sir Robert Phillimore.

it was not " What must I do ? " but " What can I do ? "

And to a nature like hers, an intuition as swift as it was unexplainable, time is a very elastic thing. Many a scheme which is either still in activity for good, or has completed its work, had at its source Mrs. Gladstone as its inspiration. She saw the need, invented the plan, found the workers, set the machinery going, and turned to something fresh.

Mr. and Mrs. Gladstone together were amongst the first and most steadfast friends of the House of Charity, still a living home of mercy and pity, in Greek Street, Soho. The Newport Market Refuge and its offspring, the Boys' Industrial School, in the Great War, as in the past, have given the army many a dauntless soldier. Mr. Gladstone, on hearing her plan, offered one hundred pounds, if she could raise nine other hundreds from her friends ; this she accomplished, and the sum of a thousand pounds started the Refuge in Newport Market, close to Seven Dials. It is now in Westminster.

Her own home at Hawarden, all through her life nearest to her heart, with its many dependent districts, found her alway, not a patroness, but a true and understanding friend, who was a wise and constant visitor, a nurse herself in many a case of illness, and ahead of her time in many of the arts of nursing. When nursing grew into a profession she did not rest till she had established a good nurse for the district, saw to her provision and her comfort, and cheered her by her sympathy.

The Lancashire Cotton Famine in 1861 gave her another opportunity for help, and in old magazines there are many reports of how she would come, discuss the questions, give a practical and practicable scheme for help, and set each place going on lines neither pauperising nor hard.

One of her tender charities was the old ladies'. Home close to the Castle, where people who had — pathetic phrase — " seen better days " were tended, comforted, amused, and constantly visited. And visitors to the Castle were sent with instructions to " make breaks for them."

Here we may give one day of her life at Hawarden, after she was eighty. She had been to early church, nearly a mile uphill, walking both ways; she had read family prayers at home; she was at her breakfast when word came that a nurse looking after typhoid patients, in a distant part of the estate, had sickened with the fever. Not a moment did she lose, and in her pony carriage she hurried off to Queen's Ferry, where the nurse was lodging. Having made full arrange-

BILLINGBEAR, BERKSHIRE

ahead of her time in many of the arts of nursing. When nursing grew into a profession she did not rest till she had established a good nurse for the district, saw to her provision and her comfort, and cheered her by her sympathy.

The Lancashire Cotton Famine in 1861 gave her another opportunity for help, and in old magazines there are many reports of how she would come, discuss the questions, give a practical and practicable scheme for help, and set each place going on lines neither pauperising nor hard.

One of her tender charities was the old ladies' Home close to the Castle, where people who had — pathetic phrase — " seen better days " were tended, comforted, amused, and constantly visited. And visitors to the Castle were sent with instructions to " make breaks for them."

Here we may give one day of her life at Hawarden, after she was eighty. She had been to early church, nearly a mile uphill, walking both ways; she had read family prayers at home; she was at her breakfast when word came that a nurse looking after typhoid patients, in a distant part of the estate, had sickened with the fever. Not a moment did she lose, and in her pony carriage she hurried off to Queen's Ferry, where the nurse was lodging. Having made full arrange-

BILLINGBEAR, BERKSHIRE

UNIV. OF
CALIFORNIA

ments, she came back to the Castle to explain to her family; then returned to the station at Queen's Ferry (two and a half miles off), and whipped the nurse off by train to Chester. Arrived there, she supported the patient up and down the long stairs at the railway station, carrying her bag and parcels in a fly with her all round Chester, in vain seeking admittance. At length, partly cajoling, partly scolding, she persuaded the Infirmary authorities to take her in; and, having seen her comfortably tucked up, she returned to the station, with a sandwich from the matron, and reached home about four o'clock. The grandchildren were coming to tea. First she prepared a stage— she had promised them charades—arranging screens, furniture, lights; then collected and arranged the rows of seats. Flew across to the Orphanage and Home of Rest to charter an audience from the inmates, among whom she placed the Prime Minister, wheedled out of his Temple of Peace; gathered the children round her in the green-room, and, after a rapid coaching and coaxing, put them through their paces—taking a prominent part herself—and somehow or other contrived to get them through fairly creditably (none of them having any turn for acting). Afterwards she presided at their tea-party, finishing up by playing spirited dances for them till it was time for them to leave. Still there remained dressing and dinner and the normal evening, till bed welcomed her to well-earned rest.

Just about the same period, after a mission held in the parish of Hawarden, she went up to sleep at the Rectory, so as to be close to the church for the final service. She had worked hard throughout the mission, which had lasted a week. It was in January, and bitterly cold. The Holy Communion was to be celebrated at 4 a.m., so that all or any might come to church before their work.

At 3.30 a.m. her son, the Rector, went to her room with a can of hot water. He knocked at the door. She opened it fully dressed for going out of doors. She had already had her cold bath.

She worked for the Institution for the Blind, for St. Mary Magdalen's in Paddington, for a preventive Home in Notting Hill; she established soup kitchens in St. George's in the East during hard winters of exceptional distress. Her doings would fill volumes, and surely do fill one volume—that of "The Lord's Book of Remembrance."

Of all her works, the Home that bears her name might be reckoned as the nearest to her heart—the one known as the Catherine Gladstone Home. It was the only free institution for convalescents in the kingdom. Begun in

1866 at Woodford, Essex, many thousands have been its guests, nursed back to health of body, and with bruised and sore spirits soothed and consoled. It is easy to go to the East End and beyond it now; it was toilsome then. But she constantly went to Woodford (the Home is now established at Mitcham), till she finally left London in 1894. She took people with her whom she could interest, sat and talked with the inmates, and with her marvellous intuition would select those whom prompt help could start afresh. Then she would set herself to enliven them, and, with a singularly brilliant touch, would play them dance music to cheer their spirits and set them singing or dancing.

Once a week Mrs. Gladstone, with Lady Frederick Cavendish, went to the London Hospital, herself saw and selected the patients, and sent them down to Woodford with words of cheer. No one who went to the Home could ever say, "No man careth for my soul."

In 1866 London was swept by a plague of cholera. Mrs. Gladstone, regardless of infection, threw herself into the work in home and hospital. In the latter, so great was the pressure that the sick had often to be laid on the floor till death vacated a bed. Mrs. Gladstone encouraged and inspired doctors and nurses, comforted the dying with words of faith, and promises of care for the orphans left desolate. These promises took much time and contrivance to fulfil, but they were fulfilled. It was then she carried off the babies rolled up in blankets. One outcome was an orphanage at Hawarden for the boys, Mrs. Tait taking the girls—in whom to her life's end she took the warmest personal interest, starting them in life, writing to them, and understanding their characters.

The Convalescent Home was really founded as a result of the cholera outbreak.

It was her constant habit to ask the matron of the Convalescent Home, "Is there any good case we can set on its feet?" No sooner was one found than she set every resource to work, till the man or woman was well started and had a full and fair opportunity; Mr. Gladstone being always ready to say, "Remember, if it's wanted, I'm good for help."

At the Home the inmates were, and are still, guests, expected to behave as such, and responding to the invitation.

One day, while busy selecting convalescents for her Home, she asked Mrs. Lyttelton[1]—, who had accompanied her to the London Hospital—to visit meanwhile in the wards. Finding herself in the men's ward, something

[1] Constance, wife of Rev. Hon. W. H. Lyttelton.

made her approach a man of singularly un-inviting aspect, so gloomy and sinister was his expression. The *Tale of Two Cities* was in his hand. "And that's what we want here," he growled. "A Revolution." "But surely," said Constance, "the cruelties and injustices of those days are past; think of all the loving-kindness there is in the world—look at Mrs. Gladstone—she brought me here." His whole face changed and softened. "Ah! Mrs. Gladstone, *she* is different." And as he spoke, the door opened, and she came in and looked round with her radiant, tender smile. "If only there were more like her . . . "

Into one pitiful field of work, the work of tenderness and compassion for the fallen, rescue and prevention work among women, Mr. and Mrs. Gladstone had thrown the full fervour of their hearts. In 1852 they met Mrs. Monsell at Naples, and planned and shared with her in the establishment of the famous and beautiful group of buildings at Clewer.

Fifty years ago they had a meeting at their house in Carlton Terrace to start the Mary Magdalen Rescue Home, later on moved to Paddington. The chief object of this Home was to shelter the babies as well as the girl mothers. This was at that time quite a new departure. They held strongly the opinion that it was the most natural as well as the most wholesome course, and often a means of regeneration to the mother.

In the streets of London they worked with tireless energy; she shrank from nothing. This is not the place to enlarge on this subject. But when walking home one night with a friend, Mr. Gladstone turned back to rescue a poor, lost créature. "But what will Mrs. Gladstone say if you take this woman home?" Mr. Gladstone turned round in surprise. "Why, it is to Mrs. Gladstone I am taking her."

Truly it could be said throughout her life, "The heart of her husband doth safely trust in her."

Helpfulness—that was the note of her character. In any difficulty, in the most impossible case, she would plan, contrive, arrange, enlist others, and never rest until the difficulty was solved and the persons put in the way of helping themselves; nay, more—supported, befriended, encouraged, till they could stand alone. Perhaps few persons were so often consulted and appealed to. It might be young girls entering on life, in the first joy of a marriage engagement; or young beauties to whom she would suggest thoughts that were unworldly. Often it would be some hard-worked London priest, toiling single-handed among his thousands and thinking, "No one cares," who found in her not only a listener but a sympathising friend; one who did not forget, but would forward his plans, and had the rare gift of setting other people to work.

During the Cattle Plague she established a whole family at the Castle, a mother and five or six children, to relieve the hard-hit gentleman farmer of interruptions and financial anxieties.

In 1893 the head mistress of a school near Tavistock, in despair how to dispose of one of her teachers—ill, poor, and friendless—as a forlorn hope wrote to Mrs. Gladstone, because she had heard of her as kind, and then to the Duchess of Bedford as wife of the landowner. From the Duchess she received a ten-pound cheque; from Mrs. Gladstone a letter: "Send her off to Hawarden to-morrow. . . ."

From the House of Charity in Soho she carried off a poor parson sick with scarlet fever, and established him in her own house in Carlton Terrace.

A Sister of Mercy's life? Yes, and besides this—

"Great duties to be greatly done"—

there was the life of a great lady, moving in

a world of parties and social claims, with a husband the foremost figure in politics, whose every interest she shared, whose health and strength she garnered.

It is hardly right to open the door of home life, yet could one know her without doing so? Hawarden Castle! How the name suggests all the charm and serenity of home! It was well said in the diary of one who came there for the first time, "Thou hast set my feet in a large room"—so fresh and sweet and spacious was the atmosphere. Her own children, her children's children, the host of nephews and nieces to whom she was a mother and gathered into the warm circle of her love, the children of old friends and any lonely soul of any class whom she could cherish—these, as well as all that was brilliant, zealous, and inspiring in the life of that day: good, or to be helped to be good, that was the essence of it all. Religion, not forced, not obtruded, but as natural and vital as fresh air was, not an adjunct of life, but life itself.

In her own devotions, in the daily Services of the Church, in many a Eucharist, did Catherine Gladstone renew her soul's life and increase the charity and the delightful gaiety of her temperament, and from the Spirit of Wisdom learn those intuitions which so rarely failed her. It seemed but natural that her last spoken words were, "I must not be late for church."

There was a something vital, tender, and wise in her spirit which lives on—

"... the actions of the just
Smell sweet and blossom in the dust."

CHAPTER VIII

REMINISCENCES

"Perfect wife and tender mother,
Scarcely shall we find another
Equal to her.
To the Almighty reverence due
She lowly tendered, friendship true
To all who knew her."

MANY thrilling experiences crowd in upon the mind as we look back across the years. Moments of intense emotion in the early hours of the morning, when a few of us would find ourselves gathered together in the Carlton Terrace house, after some kindling debate, or some crucial division. A stray Whip or so on his way back from the House, possibly Mr. George Glyn; a Secretary or an enthusiastic M.P.—Freddy and Lucy Cavendish oftenest of all, as their house was opposite ours—dropping in to rejoice or condole, to share in victory or defeat, in exhilaration or depression; some great cause lost (for the time) or won. The view across the Park from the windows of our house, in the early morning, dwells in the memory as one of singular beauty—the mass of foliage in the foreground, the towers of the Houses of Parliament and the Abbey rising above the trees, the mysterious light, the whisper of the leaves, the magic of the dawn. . . .

"And all that mighty heart is lying still."

Again there is the crowd of passionate Reformers in June 1866. Mrs. Gladstone was alone in the house, with three or four members of the family. The cheers and shouts for Mr. Gladstone grew in enthusiastic insistence. His Reform Bill, ten days earlier, had been beaten in the House of Commons, by the defection of some members of his own party. The working classes had awoken to the fact that here was a man, the first official statesman, who was ready to live or die for them. He was beaten. The Government had resigned. But in perhaps the most inspired speech ever delivered in the House of Commons: " You cannot fight against the future," he said, with a splendid sweep of his arm. " Time is on our side. The great social forces that move onward in their might and majesty, and which the tumult of our debates cannot impede or disturb —they are marshalled on our side; the banner which we now carry in this fight, though at some moment it may droop over our sinking heads, will soon again float in the eye of

Heaven, and will be borne in the hands of the united people, perhaps not to an easy, but to a certain and to a not far-distant victory."

Words worthy to rank with Lincoln's immortal speech at Gettysburg, and kindling the same torch of freedom.[1]

"Here," says Lord Morley, "the forecast was not a phrase, but a battle-cry—it revealed a cause and a man." The Government resigned office, but Mr. Gladstone's prophetic vision was realised, and the banner uplifted even sooner than he knew. The Reform Bill that became law in the following year was the fulfilment of his prophecy.

Meanwhile, on the night of June 28, the road in front of their house was blocked by an excited crowd, persistently calling on him to appear. He was absent from home. Finally the police officers sent word to Mrs. Gladstone, that if only she would show herself upon the balcony, the crowd would quietly go home. This she did, inadvertently drawing upon herself, as his representative, the passionate enthusiasm of the people.

A characteristic incident took place in Downing Street, about the year 1881, which, though trivial in itself, is worth recording for its hint of prophecy. A big official banquet

[1] "This nation, under God, shall have a new birth of freedom; that government of the people, by the people, for the people, shall not perish from the earth."

was taking place in the large dining-room, then only used on formal occasions, this being the preface to an evening party. Mr. Balfour's sisters, Eleanor and Alice, were dining quietly at No. 10 with Mrs. Gladstone and her daughters. There was a snug little room downstairs, next door to the Cabinet room, where we dined. In the evening we were sitting cosily talking round the drawing-room fire, with little consciousness of the coming party, Mrs. Gladstone, in a tea-gown, reposing on the sofa, her daughter-in-law fast asleep, on another sofa. Suddenly the door opened—"Sir Joseph and Lady Hooker,"[1] announced the butler in loud tones. The evening party had begun. The time had flown quickly. We were not even dressed. Mrs. Gladstone, awoken out of sound slumber, noiselessly melted, by another door, out of the room. Her daughters, whispering to the Balfours, "You must be hostesses," did likewise. Little did we then foresee the time, about fifteen years ahead, when Mr. Balfour, as First Lord of the Treasury, would be residing in 10 Downing Street, and would, with his sister, be receiving at an evening party—possibly the famous botanist himself—but anyway their own guests.

And the final farewell in Downing Street.

[1] Head of Kew Gardens.

That is a haunting memory, but not without its gleam of joy. It was the 12th of March. Mr. Gladstone had paid his last official visit to the Queen, and was no longer Prime Minister. He had resigned, and the last day had come. The carriage was at the door; disconsolate figures were wandering restlessly about the familiar rooms—secretaries, servants, officials; Mr. Gladstone always occupied to the very last moment; his wife bidding good-bye to faithful friends, her face sad and wistful, and, as some one remarked at the time, looking as if her mainspring was broken. As an accompaniment, a child's clear voice rang out from the staircase. This was the little granddaughter whose home was theirs so long as they lived. She had struck four the previous day, and had been decorated with a birthday wreath of flowers. Unconscious of the historic scene vibrating with emotion, in which she was sharing, she sat patiently on the stairs waiting for the start, and occupying the time in singing the Easter hymn. The Hallelujahs formed a kind of Greek chorus to the farewells. . . .

Only once again did they visit Downing Street. On June 22, 1895, news reached the *Tantallon Castle*,[1] as she drew near to England, of the defeat of the Liberal Government. A

---

[1] The ship in which we were the guests of Sir Donald Currie.

telegram from Lord Rosebery was handed to Mrs. Gladstone before we disembarked, containing an invitation to dine with him that night. It was interesting once more to see them there in the well-known rooms. Illuminated by Lord Rosebery's irresistible charm, we had a most delightful evening, the late and the present Prime Ministers being merry as boys out of school. We dined in the beautiful room, used latterly by Mr. Gladstone for Cabinet Councils (our own sitting-room now becoming—as in Lord Beaconsfield's day [1] —the Prime Minister's bedroom). And so ended, quietly and undramatically, Mr. and Mrs. Gladstone's connection with the historic building.

The spring and summer spent at Dollis Hill, after Mr. Gladstone's resignation in 1894, was a wonderfully happy and interesting time. The most fervent words of gratitude to Lord and Lady Aberdeen could never adequately express the blessing and refreshment of that perfect haven. For nearly fifteen years, it was ready on any day, at any moment, to receive them, whether their hosts were there or not. In countless letters Mrs. Gladstone relates the joy of escaping out of the turmoil;

[1] We used to invite visitors to salute the mark on the floor made by his bed.

so near to London, yet so far, peaceful as in the depths of the country. You drove from the Marble Arch three or four miles along the Edgeware Road; presently green fields and hedges took the place of shops and houses. A deep country lane on the left brought you quickly to its gates. Mr. and Mrs. Gladstone both revelled in its restfulness, in its welcoming aspect. And in 1894 it broke the sudden departure from the absorbing interest of their public life; it floated him through the trying weeks before the operation for cataract. It enabled them to entertain relations and friends, and almost literally to live out of doors. She had a way of suddenly getting whole stacks of furniture into the garden—sofas, screens, chairs, and tables. She would have been a capital foreman to the scene-shifters at a theatre. Mr. and Mrs. Chamberlain were coming one day, and, in a twinkling, the dining-room table was out under the trees, and luncheon was laid. Lady Sarah Spencer, with her specially clear voice and enunciation, often came to read aloud, while the eyes were *hors de combat*, and many and various were the delightful and interesting people that came down to visit them.

On June 24, the day the French President, Monsieur Carnot, was assassinated, a friend came down to luncheon. All the morning their

MRS. GLADSTONE AT DOLLIS HILL, WITH HER GRAND-DAUGHTER, DOROTHY DREW
1894

UNIV. OF
CALIFORNIA

little granddaughter had been busy with the funeral of a dead thrush; a cross of flowers was laid on its grave. Mr. Gladstone was asking of his guest earnest questions about the character and beliefs of the dead President: "I am so glad," he said meditatively, "that he died a Christian."

"Does he mean the thrush?" whispered the child.

About a month after the operation on Mr. Gladstone's eyes, the doctors came down to examine the sight—the spectacles were tried on, the book was opened. Mrs. Gladstone stood close to him. All were full of hope. But he could not see; he could not read the print. There was a tragic pause, broken by his voice:

"This is a blow—for the oculists."

No word of murmur passed his lips. Time proved to be the healer, and when Mr. Nettleship came later on to Hawarden, the eye from which the cataract had been removed worked perfectly for reading and writing, and the eye that had not been touched served him for all other purposes.

And now, perhaps, for a moment, I may indulge in a reminiscence of my own; for it throws some light on the way in which Mr. and Mrs. Gladstone brought up their children. He was in the Government years before any of us were born; while children, we were never conscious of him as anything out of the common; as a rising man, step by step attaining pre-eminence among his fellows. Not many years ago I was staying in a house in Westminster on the opening night of the Session. The master of the house had become a Member of Parliament. The children were in bed. Their mother woke them out of their sleep, and led them to the window and showed them the light burning in the Clock Tower. "Do you know what that light means?" she said. "It means that father is there helping to make laws for England."

It struck me at the time as a loss that our mother had not stimulated our imagination in this way. With us it was a case of a prophet not without honour save in his own country. His sun had already risen and we knew it not. The fact of his being a Cabinet Minister, foremost among his colleagues, never impressed itself upon us as any special honour or glory. It never crossed my mind that other people's fathers were not just the same. All my friends, I thought, had the same sort of father. It was a cause of wonder to me when those who came to the house, especially our cousins, treated him with awe and reverence, listening to every word that fell from his lips. Indeed, we treated him with scant respect; argued across him while he was talking; even contradicted him. Both our parents were extraordinarily simple, and never seemed conscious of occupying an exceptional plane. Whatever we learnt on this score came to us from outward sources, *e.g.* the brothers at school. In one of Lord Acton's letters he speaks of his influence as greatest on multitudes, less in society—least at home. He contrasts it with the Tennyson home: " I could not stay with the lofty entities that surround Tennyson, even when he butters toast."

It is true that, in later years, some of the Hawarden guests were half startled and shocked by the freedom of criticism that reigned in the family circle. The balance was redressed when outside the home—to the world we have always shown a united and impregnable front! But at home we discussed things almost on terms of equality.

It bored him to hear people apologetically differ: " My dearest love, I really think you are wrong." Partly in fun, he thought it more to the point to be short and sharp: " A lie !" It is impossible to forget Lord Morley's face when he first heard one of us say to Mr. Gladstone: " A lie !" And it always succeeded. It was an unfailing amusement and put every one in good humour.

I recall the very spot on the steps of the

porch by which the house is entered, where it was suddenly borne in upon me how my eyes were holden. I had been out walking with a girl friend, Margaret Leicester Warren [1] —a hereditary friendship, her parents being great friends of Mr. and Mrs. Gladstone. She paused. "You know," she said, "I think Mr. Gladstone much the greatest man in the world, and I am not sure that he is not the greatest man who ever lived."

It was an intense moment of revelation to a daughter, and not very long after the impression received its seal in a memorable conversation with Lord Acton.

Yet though love, on the part of their children, cast out fear, the attitude of their minds towards their parents was of a very different nature from that of the present generation.

The relations between one generation and another had not become nearly so strained as in these present days. There was more identity in the point of view; the spirit of investigation was more generally dormant; things were more taken for granted; traditions accepted; other people's homes were not necessarily superior to our own. "Honour your father and your mother," was accepted in the spirit and the letter. School and University experiences did not necessarily bring sever-

[1] Daughter of Lord de Tabley.

ance, or even estrangement, between mothers and sons. The deeply interesting study of the relations between one generation and another, in the present day so much discussed in novels of note, would scarcely have fitted in those days. There was too much *esprit de corps*. The tone, the standard, set by the parents was followed almost unquestioningly by their children. Their aims were the same, they saw the same vision.

How much more there is to be thought and said on this interesting subject, but it would be out of place here.

There is no doubt that Mrs. Gladstone's supreme devotion to her husband, and her profound belief in the principles that guided him, made her very impatient with those who differed from him on fundamental questions of policy.

Therefore it was but natural that, when a nephew, specially dear to her as youngest son of her cherished sister, came to Hawarden for Christmas (1894–95) and, with his irresistible smile, light-heartedly announced to the family that he had joined the Unionist ranks, she was at first greatly shocked and pained. She and her sons and daughters, in fact, felt it far more acutely than did Mr. Gladstone. One of them in particular, to whom through life he had confided his inner history, personal and political, was as utterly in the dark as the rest, though the frequency and intimacy of their intercourse had not been relaxed throughout the preceding summer. And indeed he had been the first of the clan who in 1885 bravely cast in his lot for a Parliament on College Green, and had approved of the Home Rule Bills of 1886 and 1893. This is not the time to examine his reasons, but it was more a drift than a principle—though the growing power of the proletariat made him increasingly uneasy—more personal than political. But after Mr. Gladstone's resignation, the Liberal party was at its lowest ebb; it was in dire need of the loyal service of every one of its members.

And as he came nearer to his ninetieth year, and the sands of life seemed to glide through the hour-glass with ever greater rapidity, in Mr. Gladstone's own estimation every moment of his time seemed to intensify in value. When he only, discovered, at the end of a lengthy discussion in the Temple of Peace, that the matter was already settled, the die was cast, it was not to be wondered at that he was nettled, that he resented the waste of his precious time.

It is quite true that Mr. Gladstone frequently took agreement for granted, that he mistook silence for consent, and swept his interlocutor into his own net. In matters of principle—and with him every question was brought to the touchstone of conscience—he was wont to assume that others were moved by the principles he regarded as fundamental. After his death a sheet of paper was discovered among his letters, containing a list of names. It was headed, "Those who have disagreed with me," and at its foot were words to this effect, "Good for me to remember, what notable people have differed from me." And accordingly, to those who, in all honesty, had reached conclusions contrary to his own no one could have been more trustful, more generous. On one occasion when a friend confessed to him that had he been in Parliament he could not have seen his way to support the Home Rule Bill, the quietness and gentleness with which Mr. Gladstone received the news greatly astonished his friend. When his niece,[1] referring to some backing he was according to Mr. Chamberlain—"Oh, Uncle William, you really are the most magnanimous person in the world!" "What do you mean?" he said. "Chamberlain has always been very kind to me; he has behaved ill to Ireland, but never to me." Yet Chamberlain, in 1874, had described his Election address as "the

[1] Lady F. Cavendish.

meanest document that ever proceeded from the pen of a statesman."[1] Abuse of this kind went in at one ear and, as has been well said, came out at the same.

Lord Morley has placed it on record that Mrs. Gladstone once came to his room " and said how glad she was I had not scrupled to put unpleasant points before her husband; that Mr. Gladstone must not be shielded and sheltered as some great people are, who hear all the pleasant things and none of the unpleasant. That the perturbation is but short-lived. She added, ' He is never made angry by what you say.' "

It was the belief of many people that Mrs. Gladstone was ever on the watch to soothe and quiet her husband, to persuade him to give up, to retire into private life—that he was always keen for action, for power, eager for the fight. There was an impression abroad that her one aim and idea was to induce people never to disagree with him. "*We never contradict Mr. Gladstone,*" she is supposed to have said at a dinner-party. Nothing can be further from the truth. She knew better than anyone how carefully he refrained from reading books and papers eulogistic of himself, *e.g.* he never read Lord Acton's letters to his daughter or, in the

[1] *Fortnightly Review*, Oct. 1874.

Prime Minister Series, his own *Life*, by G. W. E. Russell. But he always selected and studied inimical criticism, disagreement with his own views, as wholesome and humbling, and still more as revealing ideas that had possibly not occurred to him. 'It was he who ached for retirement, she who encouraged him to remain. To her his longing for resignation was frankly a great trial. She made no secret of it. She loved the atmosphere, the stimulus of battle; she was ever eager for the fray, and, from her own point of view, she would have longed for him to die in harness.

In July 1894 they were in Scotland, Mr. Armitstead piloting them to Pitlochry, in company with Lord Acton.

August found them once more at Hawarden, the home that had been theirs all along, where they were peacefully to end their lives. The beloved home that had been hers from her cradle to the end. Few there can be who throughout life could have been surrounded and cherished by so many members of her family, four generations of whom lived by turns at Hawarden, near her or with her.

After 1839, when not at Hagley or London or Fasque, she and Mr. Gladstone lived at the Castle, with her unmarried brother, while Henry Glynne was at the Rectory. In spite of the great financial crisis that overwhelmed the Glynnes about the year 1847, they continued to reside there, and indeed, if it had not been for Mr. Gladstone, it would probably have been necessary for Sir Stephen to sell the Castle and the whole, instead of only part of, the estate. In 1872 died her favourite brother, Henry Glynne; in 1874 came the further blow of Sir Stephen's death. Her eldest son on his uncle's death became owner of Hawarden. Mr. and Mrs. Gladstone, having a life interest in the Castle, remained in possession for the remainder of their lives—about a quarter of a century. Their son thus later on wrote of his uncle: "Hawarden can never be the same to those who remember and cherish the calm sunshine of his presence in their midst. The loss of one endowed with such rare gifts of mind, such innocence of heart and gentleness of disposition, creates a void that time can scarcely fill. Such is the feeling of his successor, after the lapse of one year from his uncle's death." The near neighbourhood of their two elder sons and their families, the holiday visits of the Wickham children and their parents, added not a little to the happiness, the pleasure, and interest of all concerned. Their eldest daughter married in 1873 E. C.

Wickham,[1] Headmaster of Wellington College. The coming of the very first grandchildren, specially that of William and Katie, was no doubt an epoch-making event. Helen entered Newnham College as a student in 1878, and left it as Vice-Principal in December 1896, giving up the work she loved to devote herself to her parents.

Herbert, the only one born to the roll of the drum in Downing Street, spent every spare moment of his time at Hawarden; he was indeed through life the light of her eyes, as is often the case with the youngest child.

It would not be possible for the daughter who with her husband[2] resided at the Castle, to describe their relations with her parents —they were too near, too sacred. She also enjoyed the inestimable privilege of never leaving her home, before or after marriage, as long as her father and mother lived, and the child who came in 1890 was the darling of the home—the sunshine of their old age— not because they loved her more than the other grandchildren, but from the mere fact of her living with them.

It was the habit of their lives to go every day to church before breakfast. They enjoyed the walk, nearly a mile uphill, in the early

[1] Afterwards Dean of Lincoln.
[2] Rev. Harry Drew, married Mary, February 2, 1886.

freshness of the morning, and winter or summer, storm or sunshine, saw them going to worship in Hawarden Church, Mrs. Gladstone scattering the path with the letters which she read on the way. Not even the early cup of tea, indispensable to most people, broke their fast.

I remember the very first sign of some diminution of strength when one day, at the age of eighty-three or eighty-four, he said:

"I am afraid I must ask you to keep Petz from coming to church with me." Petz was the favourite Pomeranian dog, immortalised by a poem in *Punch*, who lay every morning on the mat at his dressing-room door waiting for him to start. "You see, I have to throw sticks for him to pick up, and stooping every other minute to get one and then throw it is too hard work on the hill."

And so, by doctor's orders, they changed their lifelong habit and substituted Evensong for the morning service.

Well on in their eighties they breakfasted in bed, not rising till ten o'clock.

They did enjoy it!

From 1894 onwards a period of great tranquillity set in, but at no time could it be said that it was ever dull or uninteresting, or that it was without its dramatic moments.

About a year and a half before Mr. Gladstone's death, Mr. Balfour came once more. The first of his visits to Hawarden was in 1870, when he stayed for a fortnight. " He relapsed quickly into the old cosy footing—no sense of restraint or stiffness. It might have been 1870 again, as regards the old friendliness. In those days he was unknown; to-day he is the Leader of the House of Commons. The talk at dinner was lively, the late and the future Prime Ministers discussing the nightly letter to the Queen." In the 'seventies Mr. Balfour used to write to Mrs. Gladstone pretty frequently. It is a real misfortune that these letters have been lost.

In the summer of 1875, when he started on his round-the-world tour, she gave him a little gold cross for his watch-chain—it still hangs there. He was always specially drawn to her by her great qualities of heart and her raciness of speech and sense of fun.

Then there was the unexpected arrival of Li Hung Chang—an interesting and picturesque scene. But the wheels drave heavily; the afternoon was hot and drowsy; there were long pauses while he struggled to think of the right thing to say; the slowness of the interpreter and the clear voice of Gilbert Talbot[1]—then five years old—ringing through

[1] Killed in action, July 1916.

the room, "How long is this going to last?"

Li refused the honour of being carried to the dining-room, unless his host was likewise carried.

And the great shock of the sudden death in Hawarden Church of the Archbishop of Canterbury.

In October 1896 he and Mrs. Benson had crossed the Irish Channel, reaching Hawarden Castle one Saturday evening. On the Tuesday following he was borne from the church in which he had died to the station where he had arrived three days earlier, on the way to Canterbury for his burial. . . .

On Sunday morning he had been to the service at 8 a.m. At 11, we walked up to church. He passed to his rest as he knelt for the Confession; Mrs. Gladstone was next to him. Both she and Mr. Gladstone joined the funeral procession from Hawarden to Sandycroft. It was a brilliant autumn morning with snow on the ground—a solemn and a moving scene.

In 1897 the Colonial Prime Ministers, including Mr. Seddon and Sir Wilfrid Laurier, arrived at Hawarden from the four quarters of the earth. They were photographed in the garden with their host and hostess, the Old Castle forming a picturesque background.

In the year of Queen Victoria's Jubilee, the Prince and Princess of Wales came to luncheon, a visit which gave exquisite pleasure to their hosts.

In the afternoon, Mr. Gladstone started up the hill to the Old Castle with the Princess, the Prince walking with Mrs. Gladstone. On reaching the bridge over the moat, Mr. Gladstone, fresh as a three-year-old, said, "Shall we go up to the top, ma'am?" Eager for the fray, she sprang forward, but first she glanced at Mrs. Gladstone for approval. An almost imperceptible and knowing little wink was telegraphed back to her—"Too much for him," it signified. Quick as lightning and with charming tact, H.R.H. replied, "Oh, Mr. Gladstone, you quite forget my poor lame leg."

The quartette were photographed, and the following day came a letter from the Princess of Wales containing these words:

"I must write one line and thank both you and Mr. Gladstone (dear William) for the kind reception you gave us in your delightful home.

"We shall always look back with the greatest pleasure to the charming day spent with you, surrounded by your children and grandchildren, which to me was a most touching sight," etc. etc.

Many were the friends that dropped in—Lord Rosebery with his boys, Sir Arthur Godley and George Russell, H. S. Holland.

Among the signatures in the Hawarden Visitors' Book, several of which occur more than once, for the years 1894–1900, are the following:

Edward and Georgina Burne Jones, John Morley, Margaret Stepney, Algernon West, Arthur Godley, Sybil and Margaret Primrose, Ronald Leveson-Gower, Welby, L. Duchesne, Arthur C. Headlam, William Booth,[1] Aberdeen and Isabel Aberdeen, Acton, E. W. Hamilton, Evelyn de Vesci, Tweedmouth, Hugh Currie, G. Armitstead, Sarah Spencer, Randall Winton, Arthur, Hugh, and E. F. Benson, Arnold Morley, Laurence Currie, A. G. Asaph, Harry and Neil Primrose, Arthur Blomfield, E. T. Cook, Breadalbane and Alma Breadalbane, George H. Murray, Northbourne, A. J. Balfour, H. J. Tennant, Ripon and H. Ripon, Walter Phillimore, Crewe, Halifax, Wenlock, George Wyndham, John Sinclair, J. M. Carmichael, Spencer and Charlotte Spencer, J. M. C. Crum, Mary Crum, Lucy Graham Smith, etc.—with a full accompaniment of Lyttelton and Gladstone and Miss Phillimore, who devoted herself absolutely to ministering to Mrs. Gladstone, specially the last two years.

[1] The General of the Salvation Army.

And near by, at Saighton and Eaton, were the delightful George Wyndham, Lady Grosvenor, the Westminsters.

In 1895, the last voyage in the *Tantallon Castle*; in 1896, the last speech at Liverpool, pleading with all the passion of his most vigorous days for Armenia; in 1897, the final visit to London for the marriage of Princess Maud, when Lord Rosebery remarked on the intense, almost dramatic interest attached to the three historic figures—Queen Victoria, Mr. and Mrs. Gladstone—all three having lived almost throughout the nineteenth century. In September 1897, their last visit to Scotland, and in November was their last journey to the Riviera—the Aberdeens, the Actons, Mr. Armitstead, Lord and Lady Rendel, who shall say which of these was the chiefest friend and benefactor? But it was the last among these that received them, welcomed them so lovingly in the sad winter months of 1897–98, when the pain and distress of his final illness was gradually undermining his health and strength. It was in the beautiful château at Cannes that Lord and Lady Rendel sheltered them. In 1890 their son Harry had married Maud, the daughter of Lord Rendel, and no words could fitly describe the devoted love they lavished both upon Mr. and Mrs. Gladstone. From Cannes they went to Bournemouth in February 1898.

On March 18, while at Bournemouth, Mr. Gladstone learnt that his life was likely to end in a few weeks. The verdict he received with serenity and a deep sense of thankfulness. On leaving Bournemouth for Hawarden, just as he entered the train, he paused and, turning to those who were seeing him off, with quiet gravity he said, "God bless you, and this place, and the land you love."

Of Mrs. Gladstone's inner life, this book tries to give a few glimpses. Of the sorrows and losses inevitable in so long a period of time, there were three that cut her to the very quick —the death of the child already mentioned— the death of her sister in August 1857—the death of her eldest son in 1891. Other sorrows there were, the loss of brothers, parents, relations, friends. But these three were different not only in degree but in kind. One of the Lyttelton twelve,[1] then a boy of thirteen, to this hour remembers the strange, wistful, almost hungry look in her eyes as she gazed and gazed in his face, striving to recognise in him some image of his mother—a look that impressed, haunted, yet baffled him, significant of an emotion too deep and too poignant for him to fathom.

It was no ordinary link that bound these

[1] Albert Victor.

[*Numa Blanc Fils*
MR. AND MRS. GLADSTONE AT CANNES
1898

two sisters. Of Mary it was once said that always "she made a sunshine in a shady place."[1] On entering a room it was impossible not to be aware of her presence, such light and sweetness did it bring to the atmosphere. Possibly something of the beauty of her disposition, the high sense of honour and of duty, the capacity for love and sacrifice, may be guessed from the lives and characters of her children, reflected indeed in the Lyttelton twelve.

As we have already seen, these two sisters were one in thought and mind, and the rending asunder of the one from the other signified a wound that no time would heal. "Oh, if I were to see you in this state," said the dying sister, as she gazed at Catherine with infinite love and longing, "*I think it would break my heart.*" And again, "I cannot possibly imagine you on earth without me."

It was soon after the birth of Alfred, the youngest of the twelve, that Mary's health began to fail, and for many weeks Catherine was at Hagley, taking a large share in the nursing— there were no professional nurses in those days. In her own words, written at the time: "After receiving the Holy Communion her calmness was extraordinary, and she even

[1] Spenser's *Faerie Queene*.

said to me she ' would not wish to come back again.'

'O Lord, my God, do Thou Thy Holy Will.
I will lie still.'

All discomposure and anxiety had left her. The Blessed Sacrament was life and sustenance, carrying her through the dark Valley of the Shadow of Death. She had left all her cares to Him who careth for her."

The peace and beauty of the last days, the little traits of fun that carried her through the suffering, the gratitude, and almost enjoyment of any little alleviation, the look of fulfilment on her face after death, lifted the infinite sense of love and loss, on the part of those that watched and mourned, to the highest spiritual level. And the maiming and crushing of her heart brought out special sweetness and endurance in the sister who was left. But there is no doubt it was one of those heart-searching sorrows from which there is, in this world, no real recovery. Pain lives with us and becomes part and parcel of our being; we grow accustomed to its burden and its sting. But this in no way signifies the healing of the wound, and with Mrs. Gladstone it was life-long. Many, many years later she wrote to her daughter, describing the pain she had to endure while a friend, sitting by her side at a dinner-party, persisted in speaking of Lady

Lyttelton, questioning her of her sister—and how she could not bear it.

It is sometimes thought that old age brings gradual immunity from suffering, that its edge is blunted, that the feeling of loss is blurred. This may be so, but it was by no means the case with Mrs. Gladstone in 1891. From the moment her son became ill in 1890, " she went heavily as one that mourneth." Anyone would feel she was changed, that she carried a heart sorely wounded; the buoyancy was gone, brave though she might be in trying to hide her sorrow.

Some time after his death, her daughter one day discovered some photographs of him in a drawer in her mother's room. She asked leave to take them away and get them framed and placed on her writing-table. "You will think me such a coward," she said, with an inexpressible look of pain, " but I keep them hidden on purpose, because I have not the courage to look at them."

The death of her husband was so different; it did not seem to part them—she felt him so near to her.

CHAPTER IX

VIA CRUCIS—VIA LUCIS

IT is hardly possible to convey any accurate idea of the great ocean of sympathy and loving-kindness that flowed in from every part of the world during those last weeks—thousands, even millions, seemed to watch round his death-bed.

" From every rank in social life came outpourings in every key of reverence and admiration. People seemed—as is the way when death comes—to see his life and character as a whole, and to gather up in his personality, thus transfigured . . . all the best hopes and aspirations of their own highest moments." [1]

It was a time of great suffering, but it was a time of great glory. It was a way of sorrows, but it was a way of victory. And all through those weeks she was near him, cheering, fortifying, sweetening the atmosphere. She herself was not well, but all through his illness her spirit rose to a high plane of self-forgetfulness,

[1] Lord Morley.

and she devoted herself absolutely to soothe and minimise his pain.

Among the many scenes of pathetic interest, the farewell visits of those dear to him, there is one that none could ever forget who witnessed it. The cherished boy who bore his name, and who seventeen years later was, on the field of battle, to consecrate it anew, came down to the Castle to receive the farewell blessing.

Will was then an Eton boy of thirteen. By his father's death seven years earlier he had become heir to Hawarden. Mrs. Gladstone was seated close to her husband. With a gesture of infinite tenderness she drew him into her arms, and holding him close she gathered up all her strength, physical and mental; she spoke to him in the most wonderful way of his father and his mother, and the love he bore them; she spoke of the past and of all that had been suffered and sacrificed for Hawarden by his grandfather; she spoke of the future and of his own great duties as owner of the estate, of his responsibilities, of the great example he was to follow. With her dying husband hardly conscious by her side, she poured out to the boy, who listened so intently, her love for him, her hope for him, her belief in him. . . .

In May came some of his nearest friends and

relations. Lord Rosebery came; Mr. Morley came; Lady Stepney and her daughter; George Russell and H. S. Holland; Bishop Wilkinson to administer the Holy Communion. Mrs. Benson came; her words written to one of her sons gives her own vivid impression.

"HAWARDEN CASTLE, *May* 1, 1898.

"We have had a wonderful time. Mrs. Gladstone, though older, more worn, has just begun to realise that he cannot recover. She wept when she told me this, but she was full of other people as usual—very full of us, and of the last time she had seen me here.

"It is most pitiful, but also magnificent. . . . He is cast down and depressed, and suffers sadly at times. . . . His faith has never failed, and it is his uselessness which seems to weigh on his mind. . . . They hope he sleeps a good deal. Mrs. Wickham said he seems 'communing with God'—and from time to time he breaks out into his favourite hymn, 'Praise to the holiest in the height' (only he likes best to say 'highest'). He blesses everyone who comes near him.

"The evening drew on and I had not seen him, when suddenly Mary Drew came to me and said, 'Come quickly. I have told him you were here, and he says he will see you at once—but, he said, I can't talk.' We ran to his room.. It was very dark—he always will have it so—and in the middle with his back to the light he lay in a long chair; the dim light fell on his splendid head.

"I knelt by him and took his hand. M. D., said, 'Here is Mrs. Benson.' He took my hand and kissed it, and said, 'God bless you. Will you give me your prayers?' I said how he always had them—how I prayed continuously for him. 'Nobody,' he said, 'needs your prayers more than the poor sinner who lies here before you.' This rang out in his magnificent voice—no alteration in that; then he went on, 'I often think of your husband; perhaps he pities me now.' I said, 'He loves you now as he did always,' and I kissed his hand which was still holding mine. He blessed me again and I came away. You will know all it was—sight and sound and words. . . .

"Their kindness and thought and tenderness are indescribable. I saw her again yesterday, and thanked her as well as I could. They tell me that what helps him most is anything that is said of his in any way *helping the world*. I am sure if the world saw what I did they could be 'helped' indeed. . . . God give him his release soon."

There is no need to describe here the very last

sacred days and hours. They are written large on the hearts of men.

With his wife and children all around, in the early morning of Ascension Day, without a pang, he ceased to breathe. "Nature outside —wood and wide lawn, and cloudless, far-off sky—shone at her fairest."

Mrs. Gladstone, exhausted with the long watching, half an hour later, quiet and beautiful as of old, fell into dreamless sleep. I still see her in the last historic scenes of her life—on every great occasion, with undiminished spirit, she rose to the call. Two scenes in particular abide in the memory.

On May 22, a fatal accident occurred in one of the Estate Collieries. Mrs. Gladstone, herself widowed only two days earlier, at once went to the cottage, and after speaking to the dead collier's wife in words of tenderest understanding and sympathy, she knelt down on the floor beside her, and prayed aloud a spontaneous, extempore prayer, a humble intercession expressed in the simplest words.

A few days later, early in the morning, Mrs. Gladstone received the Holy Communion in Hawarden Church, as the coffin, under its white pall, lay before the Altar. After the service we drove in an open carriage in the funeral procession, through the Park, with its glory of spring blossoms, and its black masses of

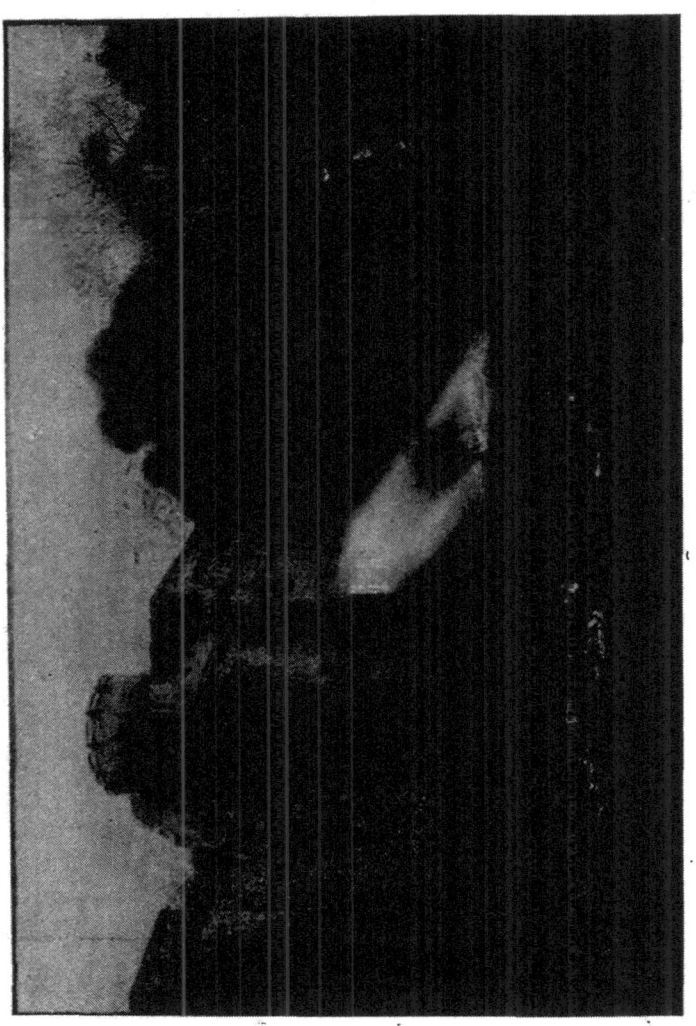

HAWARDEN CASTLE BY NIGHT
MAY 19, 1898, 4 A.M.

From a drawing by C. J. Staniland, R.I.

people, thousands and thousands, from Manchester and Liverpool and other manufacturing towns. Like another great lady [1] twelve years later, she forgot everything but the thought of giving pleasure to the people, as she bowed from side to side all the way to the station.

As she entered the great west door of the Abbey, the vast concourse of people, seated tier above tier on each side of the nave, spontaneously rose as she walked slowly up the centre. "She went in like a widow, she came out like a bride"—so did the whole ceremony uplift and inspire her. The scene at the grave was indeed memorable. As the last solemn strains of the Dead March were dying away— Mrs. Gladstone, a noble and pathetic figure, by the open grave, gazing down upon the coffin of her husband—the Prince of Wales, afterwards King Edward VII., was seen to approach. Bending down, he reverently kissed her hand; his example was followed by the other pallbearers — Prince George (now King), Lord Salisbury, Lord Rosebery, Mr. Balfour, the Duke of Rutland, Lord Spencer, Lord Kimberley, Sir William Harcourt, Lord Rendel, Mr. Armitstead, and Lord Pembroke (who represented Queen Victoria). To each one of them, as they bent down, she spoke some appropriate

[1] Queen Alexandra.

word, showing far more self-control than any of these deeply moved friends.¹

"The congregation that filled the Abbey, the simplicity of dress, the unostentation of the ceremonial, resembled the funeral of a village hero, in his own parish church. Only the parish was the Empire, and the mourners were the representatives and rulers of the world. The most beautiful sight was the loving wife, who for sixty years had ministered to the dead man. Her sweet, patient, hopeful face was a homily and a solace to all who saw it."

And another wrote: "It was all so beautiful and moving—your darling mother thanking the pall-bearers—how wonderful she was. The most touching thing of all was when she walked down the nave, leaning on the arms of her two sons, and as she passed she smiled at the faces she knew—everybody cried at this —her being able so to forget herself, and remember others in the most crushing moment of her life."¹

Then there is Lord Morley's unforgettable description of the mourning nations—France, America, Russia, Italy, Greece, Norway, Denmark, the Balkan Provinces—nations that had struggled or were struggling to be free: "It was not at Westminster only that his

¹ Charlotte Ribblesdale.

praise went forth—famous men have the world for their tomb—in foreign lands a memorial of them is graven on the hearts of men. No other statesman on our famous roll has touched the imagination of so wide a world. . . ."

Before she returned to Hawarden, Lord Rosebery came to her, bringing his two boys to be blessed by her. Only two years of loneliness were to pass. She left London the same day —it was typical of her unself-consciousness that she never looked at a paper, never once asked that the account of the historic scenes should be read to her. She lived her quiet life, physically and mentally, very gradually failing. Only once did she leave Hawarden again, taking a house at Penmaenmawr in the autumn of 1898, and paying a farewell visit to Penrhyn Castle. On October 5, 1899, the Duke of Westminster, in her presence, laid the first stone of St. Deiniol's Library—it was part of the Nation's memorial to Mr. Gladstone. Mrs. Gladstone, the previous day, had cut the first sod. Thus were these two lifelong friends together in their last public act. Their intercourse had at one time been shadowed by political differences. But in the end they were associated in a ceremony, the object of which was homage to Mr. Gladstone. The Duke only lived a few more weeks. She survived him by six months. She was chiefly in the company those last two years of her daughters and daughters-in-law, her nieces, and most intimate friends; and the frequent presence of her sons and grandchildren threw light and joy on the path she now trod alone. She much preferred men to women, and would often have felt a sense of boredom had not others made special journeys to see her— Lord Rosebery, H. S. Holland, Sir Arthur Godley, George Russell. This tenderness of thought for her on the part of the younger generation greatly cheered and pleased her. Hardly a day passed, after May 1898, without bringing her a word from George Russell. He loved her as a son, and never lost a chance of cheering or amusing her with some little word he had heard or read, or something he had seen, concerning her husband. As has been already said she appeared to have a sense of his nearness, almost a sense of his presence seemed to be granted to her, and there was little feeling of severance during the two years that separated them. The books she loved best were the Biographies written by Mr. Justin M'Carthy and Sir T. Wemyss Reid. These were read to her over and over again, and the sermons on Mr. Gladstone by her two sons-in-law, the Dean of Lincoln and Harry Drew; Edward Talbot and Arthur

Lyttelton, her nephews, and H. S. Holland, were rivers of refreshment to her.

The ministrations of the Rector, her eldest surviving son, the presence of the wife and children of her loved eldest son, who after the death of Mr. Gladstone took up their residence at the Castle, all this tended to vary and brighten the days of waiting. Many charming "Sayings of the Children"[1] might enliven these pages. But the shadows are now lengthening, and her life draws near to its close. With her unconquerable will and her vitality of spirit, it was hard through increasing weakness to drop, one by one, her activities, her responsibilities, her businesses. There comes a time in most lives, where the father and mother live long, when the relation between parents and children becomes, in some measure, reversed. With him it had been not only an easy task, but one that had called forth his deepest gratitude, to hand over his possessions, to leave his affairs and even his indomitable will in the hands of his children, and especially in those of Harry, his most trusted son. But to her it was difficult to give in, to give up. She still struggled to fulfil her accustomed duties, the little ministrations that she loved to bestow on all that needed them. It was the habit of her life. To the end she strove to write letters.

[1] By Pamela Glenconner.

We will not dwell on the last of her days on earth. It is life, not death, that matters. Gradually she became less and less conscious of the world—there was little or no suffering, and on the afternoon of June 14, the eager spirit passed, without struggle, to its rest. . . .

"I desire to be buried" Mr. Gladstone had written "where my wife may also lie."

And so it came to pass that burial in the great Abbey, by the side of her husband, was granted to her. No one who was present on the early morning of June 19 will forget the Service at St. Faith's. The coffin had been brought from Hawarden to Westminster Abbey on the preceding day. It had rested in the Chapel of St. Faith's during the night, with its white pall and burning tapers and the flowers that she loved; the Cross at its head, the kneeling Sisters, who had watched all night, the solemn Requiem. . . .

A few hours later, with the same solemn service, the same glorious music, the same mourners—family, children and grandchildren, friends, statesmen, and many others, high and low, rich and poor—we stood once more around that same open grave, and to many the thought must have occurred that this was more a wedding than a funeral.

"Lovely and pleasant were they in their lives, and in their death they were not divided."

THE GLYNNE FAMILY

Sir STEPHEN GLYNNE (8th Bart.) = Hon. MARY NEVILLE, daughter
1780–1815. (1806) 2nd Lord BRAYBROOKE, 1786–1854.

```
├── STEPHEN (9th Bart.) 1807–1874.
│
├── HENRY = Hon. LAVINIA LYTTELTON (1843) and had issue, all of whom died unmarried except
│   └── GERTRUDE = GEORGE, Lord PENRHYN (1875) and has issue.
│
├── CATHERINE = WILLIAM E. GLADSTONE (1839).
│   │
│   ├── WILLIAM HENRY = Hon. GERTRUDE STUART (1864) and has issue.
│   │
│   ├── Rev. STEPHEN EDWARD = ANNIE WILSON (1885) and has issue.
│   │
│   ├── HENRY NEVILLE = Hon. MAUD RENDEL (1890).
│   │
│   ├── CATHERINE JESSY, b. 1845, d. 1850.
│   │
│   ├── HERBERT JOHN (Viscount Gladstone) = DOROTHY PAGET (1901).
│   │
│   ├── AGNES = Rev. E. C. WICKHAM (1873) and has issue.
│   │
│   ├── MARY = Rev. HARRY DREW (1886) and has issue.
│   │
│   └── HELEN (Vice-Principal of Newnham College).
│
└── MARY = GEORGE, Lord LYTTELTON (1839).
    │
    ├── MERIEL SARAH = JOHN GILBERT TALBOT (1860) and has issue.
    │
    ├── LUCY CAROLINE = Lord FREDERICK CAVENDISH (1864).
    │
    ├── CHARLES GEORGE = Hon. MARY CAVENDISH (1875) and has issue.
    │
    ├── ALBERT VICTOR.
    │
    ├── NEVILLE GERALD, G.C.B. = KATHARINE STUART WORTLEY (1883) and has issue.
    │
    ├── GEORGE WILLIAM SPENCER, C.B., d. 1913.
    │
    ├── LAVINIA = EDWARD STUART TALBOT (Bishop of Winchester) (1870) and has issue.
    │
    ├── MARY CATHERINE, d. 1875.
    │
    ├── ARTHUR (Bishop of Southampton) = KATHLEEN CLIVE, and has issue.
    │
    ├── ROBERT HENRY = EDITH SANTLEY (1884).
    │
    ├── EDWARD = CAROLINE WEST (1888) and has issue.
    │
    └── ALFRED = (1) LAURA TENNANT (1885) (2) EDITH BALFOUR (1892) and has issue.
```

INDEX

Aberdeen, Lord and Lady, 215, 259, 277.
Aboyne, Lord, 11.
Acland, Sir Henry, letter from, 161.
Acton, Lady, 109, 277.
Acton, Lord, 229, 264, 268, 269, 277; his estimate of Gladstone's oratory, 232; quoted, 263; *Letters* quoted, 241 n.
Afghan Boundary dispute, 171.
Ailsa, Lady, 177 and n. 1.
Alexander, Bp., quoted, 155-6.
Alfred, Prince, 68.
Alice, Princess, 66, 94.
Alix of Hesse (Empress of Russia), 100, 191.
Anson, Gen., 143.
Argyll, Duchess of, death of, 175-6.
Argyll, Duke of, letters from, 148, 176, 193.
Armitstead, Mr., 115 and n. 1, 269, 277.
Asquith, Mrs. (Margot Tennant), letter from, 191.
At Sundry Times, 114-15.
Audley End, 5, 15.

Balfour, A. J., 86, 257; Gladstone's affection for, 238; at Hawarden, 273.
Barnard, Sir H., 144.
Bathurst, Lord, 16.
Battersea, Lord and Lady, 101.
Bellairs, Miss Eleanor, 115.
Belvoir Castle, 69.
Benson, Abp., letter from, 166; death of, 167 n., 192-3, 274.
Benson, Mrs., 199; letter on Mrs. Gladstone's last illness, 284-5.
Blücher, 129.
Books read, 36-7, 43-4.
Brabazon, Lady, 28, 38.
Braybrooke, Lord, 89.
Bright, Jacob, 224-5.
Bright, John, letter from, 175.

Brooke family, 15, 31.
Brownlow, Lady, 106.
Bryce, Lord, letter from, 164.

Cambridge, Duke of, 104; friendship with Mrs. Gladstone, 14.
Canning, Lady, letter from, 140.
Canning, Lord, 20, 65, 139, 144-6.
Carlisle, Lady, 132.
Carlton House Terrace, 38, 254-5.
Carnot, President, 260-1.
Catherine Gladstone Home, The, 246-7.
Cattle plague anecdote, 251.
Cavendish, Lady (Lady Frederick), 204, 226 and n., 247, 254, 267; letter to, 76.
Cavendish, Lord Frederick, 79, 254; murder of, 165-6, 238.
Chamberlain, Joseph, 260, 267; cited, 63.
Chaplin, H., 159-60.
Charitable undertakings, 243-4, 246, 248.
Chatham, Lady, 5.
Chess, 37.
Childers, H., 104.
Cholera epidemic, 1, 247.
Church in its relation to the State, The, 7, 22, 45, 63.
Churchill, Lord Randolph, 105.
Clark, Sir Andrew, 83, 237 and n.
Claughton, Bp., 104, 106.
Cobden, R., 132-3.
Cobham, Mary, 169.
Coleridge, J. T., 42.
Colonial Prime Ministers at Hawarden, 274.
Cook and the Captain, The, 237.
Coutts, Angela Burdett, 137 and n.
Cowper, Lady. *See* Palmerston.
Cowper, William, 153.
Currie, Sir Donald, 172 n.

Dalhousie, Lord, 66.

295

Dalmeny, 16–17.
de Falbe, Mme, 105.
de Rothesay, Lady Stuart, 11.
de Tabley, Lady, 44.
de Tabley, Lord, 20.
Delamere, Lady, letter of, 127–30.
Delane, J. T., letter from, 180.
Denison, Archdeacon, 137.
Derby, Lord, 127.
Disraeli, B., 125, 127.
Dollis Hill, 259–60.
d'Orléans, Duc, 10.
Douglas, Lord, 9–10 and n. 1.
Downing Street party anecdote, 256–7.
Doyle, Sir Francis, 20, 33.
Dress fashions, 181–4.
Drew, Dorothy Mary Catherine, 115, 258, 261, 271 and n. 3.
Drew, Rev. Harry, 271 and n. 2.
Drew, Mary, letter of, to Lady F. Cavendish, 76.
Dufferin, Lord, letter from, 185.
Durdans, The, 111.

Edward, Prince (Eddy), 103; death of, 113–14.
Ellen Middleton, 238.
Ellenborough, Lord, 145.
Escrich, 37.

Fasque, 34.
Frederick William IV., King of Prussia, 45.
Frere, Sir Bartle, 104 and n.

Garibaldi, Gen., letter from, 151.
George, Prince, 189, 287.
Gladstone, Agnes, 66–9.
Gladstone, Catherine, ancestry of, 1–4; childhood and education, 5–9; in Paris, 9–12; home life, 13–15; in Scotland, 16–17; London gaieties, 17–18; in Naples and Rome, 20–1; Mr. Gladstone's first proposal, 22; return to London, 24; engaged, 24–9; married, 30 ff.; birth of her eldest son, 41; death of her child Catherine Jessy, 73–4, 278; rescue work, 249–50; death of her sister, 278–80; Lancs. cotton famine, 95 ff., 244; cholera epidemic, 1, 247; *Pembroke Castle* trip (1883), 172 and n.; visit to Italy, 184; golden wedding, 187;
death of her eldest son, 278, 281; specimen day of her old age, 244–6; in her husband's last illness, 282–6; his funeral, 286–8; failing health, 289 ff.; death and funeral, 292; her affection for her sister, 18, 26, 36, 54; position in her home, 19; relations with her husband, 28, 68, 219, 230, 235–6, 265, 268, 281; watchful care of him, 208, 221–2; book of extracts, 7–8; record work of her children, 53–4; appearance of, 18–19, 202.
Gladstone, Harry, 92 and n., 277.
Gladstone, Helen, 29–30, 105, 271.
Gladstone, Herbert, 92 and n., 165, 271.
Gladstone, Jessy, 68, 72–4, 278.
Gladstone, Rev. Stephen, 68, 71; letter from, quoted, 79.
Gladstone, W. E.—meets the Glynnes in Naples and Rome, 20–1; first proposal, 22; accepted, 24; speech on the Corn Laws, 46–7; as President of Board of Trade, 48; shooting accident, 52, 136; enters the Cabinet, 58–9; resigns on Maynooth grant, 62–6; M.P. for Oxford (1847), 131 n.; European journey for a friend (1849), 71–2; death of his child (1850), 73; Chancellor of the Exchequer (1853), 126, 137; re-election, 137–8; the Budget (1860), 147; political campaigns —Newcastle, Midlothian, etc., 116 ff.; Reform Bill (1866), 255–6; Prime Minister (1868), 151; political achievement, 81; resignation (1875), 82 ff.; second time Premier (1880), 163; popular sentiments towards, 164–5; Bingley Hall speech (1888), 178–80; cataract, 261; old age, 272; at Cannes, 277; at Bournemouth, 277–8; fatal illness, 277, 278, 282 ff.; death of, 195 ff., 286; funeral, 286–9; his orderly habits, 28; domestic interests, 58; trustfulness, 209; estimate of, 231 ff.; his oratory, 232; Millais portrait, 107; Biographies, 230, 290; letter to Lord Lyttelton quoted, 233–4; *The Cook and the Captain*, 237; three sleepness nights, 238.

INDEX

Gladstone, W. G. C., 283.
Gladstone, W. H., 41, 44, 58, 63, 89; estimate of, as a boy, 71; engagement of, 157; death of, 278, 281.
Gladstone family, the, 25; home life of, 263-5.
Glenconner, Lady, 110 and nn., 291 n.
Glyn, George, 254.
Glyn, Sir John, 3.
Glynne, Lady (Mary Neville), 1-2, 4-5, 8-9, 33, 135 and n. 3.
Glynne, Henry (brother), 6, 12, 16, 29; marriage of, 59-60; death of, 270.
Glynne, Mary. *See* Lyttelton, Lady.
Glynne, Sir Stephen (father), 1-3, 4, 26.
Glynne, Sir Stephen (brother), 6, 10 and n. 2, 11, 35; death of, 155 n., 270.
Glynnese Glossary, 23 n. 1, 55, 211 and n. 1, 225.
Godley, Sir Arthur, 276, 290.
Gordon, Gen., 170.
Graham, Sir James, letter from, 147.
Granville, Lord, 102, 108; luncheon party to, 222-3.
Grenville, the Rev. and Hon. G. N., 6 n., 12, 31.
Grenville, Thomas, 12, 25, 44 and n., 65; letter from, 130.
Grosvenor, Lady, 110.
Grosvenor, Hugh, 169.
Guizot, 69.

Hagley, 15, 31, 59, 134.
Hamilton, Duchess of, 10.
Hamilton, Duke of, 20.
Harcourt, Abp., 26.
Harcourt, Col., 17 and n. 2.
Harcourt, Lord, quoted, 217.
Harcourt, Sir Wm., 197.
Harris, Lord, 20.
Harrison, Frederic, letter from, 194.
Hartington, Lord, 108, 213.
Hawarden—Visitors' Book, 276; St. Deiniol's Library, 239.
Hawarden Estate, 3; colliery accident, 285.
Hawarden parish, 12-13; New Church, 59.
Heathcote, Mr. and Mrs., 16.
Heber, Bishop, 8.

Herbert, Mrs., 147.
Herbert, Sidney, 91.
Hesse, Princesses of, 100, 191.
Holland, Rev. H. Scott, 276, 284, 290; quoted, 209 and n. 1.
Home Rule split, 174 ff.
Hook, Dr., 59.
Hooker, Sir Joseph and Lady, 257.
Hope, A. J. B., 58-9.
Hunt, Holman, letter from, 169.

Indian Mutiny, the, 140 ff.

Jarnac, Mme, 69-70.

Keate, Dr., 43.
Kiel Harbour opening, 117.

Lancashire cotton famine, 95 ff., 244.
Lawley, Jane, 29.
Lawrence, Sir H., 144.
Lefevre, J. Shaw, 65.
Leinster, Lord, 177.
Leopold, Prince (Duke of Albany), death of, 166.
Li Hung Chang, 273-4; letter from, 193.
Liddon, Canon, letter from, 155.
Lincoln, Abraham, quoted, 256 and n.
Lister, Mr. and Mrs., 16.
Liszt, Abbé, 9.
Lloyd, Gen., 142.
Lovelace, Lady, quoted, 210-11.
Lyttelton, Dowager Lady, 61, 62, 88 and n. 3; letter from, 152.
Lyttelton, Lady, 6, 7, 11, 14, 19, 42; engagement, 26; marriage, 30; children of, 54; at Hagley, 134; characteristics of, 18; death of, 278-280.
Lyttelton (George), Lord, 26-7, 30.
Lyttelton, Albert Victor, 278 and n.
Lyttelton, Alfred, 169 and n. 1, 279.
Lyttelton, Mrs. Alfred (Laura Tennant), 172 and n.; quoted, 220.
Lyttelton, Arthur, 107.
Lyttelton, Constance, 248-9.
Lyttelton, Katharine, quoted, 210.
Lyttelton, Lavinia (Lavinia Glynne), 59-60.
Lyttelton, Lucy, 88.
Lyttelton, Mary (niece), 212 and n.
Lyttelton, Meriel, 42, 44, 88.

INDEX

Macaulay, Lord, 22.
Mahony, Pierce. *See* O'Mahony.
Manning, Cardinal, 22, 42, 58–9, 61; letters from, 136, 187.
Marie Antoinette, 70.
Maynooth, 63–6.
Melbourne, Lord, 209.
Midlothian campaign, 164, 221–2.
Monsell, Mr., 249.
Morley, Lord, 263, 284, quoted, 63, 178–9, 231–2, 256, 268, 282, 288–9; letter from, 200; estimate of his *Life of W. E. Gladstone*, 230 and *n*. 1.
Morpeth, Lord, 132.

Napoleon's charger, 4.
'Nebuchadnezzar,' 226.
Neill, Brig.-Gen., 144.
Neville, Mrs. Chas., 89.
Neville, Grey, 89–90.
Neville, Henry, 89–90.
Neville, Mary. *See* Glynne.
Neville, Mirabel, 90 and *n*. 2.
Newcastle, Duke of, 20; letters from, 138, 139.
Newman, Cardinal, letter from, 158.
Newnham College, 107.
Nicholas, Emperor of Russia, 61–2, 191.
Northcote, Sir Stafford, 65 and *n*. 3, 170; letters from, 137, 151.

O'Mahony, The, letter from, 189.
Outram, Lady, 141–2.

Palmerston, Lady (Lady Cowper), 135 and *n*. 2; letter from, 153.
Parnell, C. S., 113; the divorce case, 188.
Paul, Herbert, 113.
Peel, Arthur, 113.
Peel, Sir Robert, 42, 44, 51, 62–3, 69–70; the Corn Laws, 46–8; his estimate of Gladstone, 50–1.
Pembroke, Lady, 106.
Pembroke Castle trip, 172.
Penrhyn, Gertrude, Lady, 60.
Perceval, Mr., 137–8.
Petz, 272.
Phillimore, Mr. 52.
Phillimore, Lucy, *In Memoriam* by, cited, 242.
Phillimore, Sir R., 20, 172.
Phœnix Park murders, 165.
Platof, 129.

Primrose, Lady Peggy, 111.
Primrose League anecdote, 115.
Prince Consort, 44, 92–3.
Princess Royal, 51, 99; letter from, 188.
Prison dullness anecdote, 205–7.
Public Worship Regulation Act, 154–6.
Pusey, Dr., letter from, 181.

Recollections of an Irish Judge, 56–7.
Reeve, Henry, quoted, 34.
Reid, Sir R. (Lord Loreburn), 154.
Rendel, Lord and Lady, 184, 277.
Rescue work, 249–50.
Ribblesdale, Lady, 220.
Ribblesdale, Lord, 205.
Richmond, Sir Wm., letters from, 192, 196, 198.
Ripon, Lord, 49, 50.
Robert Elsmere, 109.
Roberts, Sir F. (Earl Roberts), 103–104.
Rogers, Samuel, 24, 26; entertaining the Church, 57; letter from, 136.
Rosebery, Lord and Lady, 16, 17.
Rosebery, Lady, death of, 111–12.
Rosebery, Lord, 259, 276, 284, 289, 290; cited, 221, 277.
Ruskin, John, 161–3.
Russell, George W. E., 276, 284, 290; letters from, 171, 174; cited, 237.
Russell, Lord and Lady John, 46, 87–8.
Ryan, Sir Charles, 221.

Saighton, 110.
St. Leonards dancing incident, 211.
Sandringham, 102 ff.
Schlüter, Auguste, letter from, 216.
Selwyn, Bishop, 42–3.
Sheil, Irish orator, 56.
Spencer, Lady Sarah, 260.
Stanley, Lord, 45, 49, 56.
Stanley, Lady Mary (Lady Mary Grosvenor), 160 and *n*.
Stanmore, Lord (Sir Arthur Gordon), letter from, 172.
Stepney, Lady, 284.
Stuart, Prof., 113.
Stuart, Gertrude, 157.
Sutherland, Duchess of, 45, 89 *n*. 1, 99.
Swansea, 116.

INDEX

Talbot, Gilbert, 273 and *n.*
Talbot, Mrs. E. S. (Lavinia Lyttelton), 211-13.
Tantallon Castle, 258, 277.
Tennant, Laura. *See* Lyttelton, Mrs. Alfred.
Tennant, Margot. *See* Asquith, Mrs.
Tennyson, Lord, 99, 150, 177; letters from, 159, 181; home life of, 263.
Tennyson, Hallam, 159-60.
Thirlwall, Bishop, 26.
Times, The, 108-9.
To Two Sister Brides, quoted, 33.

Victoria, Queen, visits Hawarden, 14; coronation of, 17; friendliness with Mrs. Gladstone, 41, 58, 66, 68, 88; sentiments towards Mr. Gladstone, 93; family life, 62; death of the Prince Consort, 93-5; interest in Lancashire cotton famine, 96; letters from, 157, 166, 189.

Wales, Prince of (Edward VII.), 51, 66-8, 71, 105; illness (1871), 99; at Duke of Albany's funeral, 167; letter from, 168; at Hawarden, 275; at Mr. Gladstone's funeral, 287.
Wales, Prince of (present), 52.
Wales, Princess of (Queen Alexandra), 99; entertains the Gladstones at Sandringham, 102, 107; visits Hawarden, 275; letters from, 191, 195, 275.
Warren, Margaret Leicester, 264.
Watts, G. F., letter from, 190.
Wedding-ring incident, 221.
Wellington, Duke of, 41, 42, 45, 50, 61; desire to resign his commission, 51.
Wenlock, Lady, 9.
Wenlock, Lord, 17.
Westminster, Duke of, 289; letters from, 160, 165, 169, 177.
Wickham, Rev. E. C., 270-1.
Wickham, W. C., 213-14.
Wilberforce, Bishop Samuel, letters from, 153-4.
Wilkinson, Bishop, 284.
Woodford journey anecdote, 207.
Woolner, Thos., letter from, 150.
Wyndham, George, 110 and *n.* 1, 277.
Wyndham, Percy, 110 and *n.* 3.
Wynn, Sir Watkin, 30.

Zouche, Lord, 20.

PRINTED BY
MORRISON AND GIBB LIMITED
EDINBURGH

Lightning Source UK Ltd.
Milton Keynes UK
UKHW020642010522
402320UK00003B/25